FINISHING
the
FIGURE

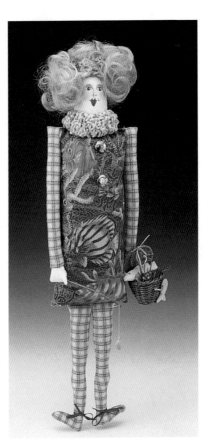

DOLL COSTUMING ▪ EMBELLISHMENTS ▪ ACCESSORIES

SUSANNA OROYAN

C&T PUBLISHING

© 2001 Susanna Oroyan
Developmental Editors: Barbara Konzak Kuhn and Joan Cravens
Technical Editor: Sara Kate MacFarland
Front and Back Cover Design: Kristen Yenche
Book Design and Design Direction: Kristen Yenche
Production Assistant: Kirstie L. McCormick
Production Coordination: Diane Pedersen
Illustrator: Tom Oroyan © C&T Publishing
Front Cover Photographs (clockwise from top left): Dorothy Hoskins, *Japanese Dancer*, 20 inches, resin. Photo by Pauline Chamness. Retagene Hanslik, *Elliott*, 18 inches, Cernit. Photo by Alan Hanslik. Dmitry Zhurilkin, *It's Time to Eat Rice*, 37 cm, splint. Photo by Viktor Chernishov. Patti Medaris Culea, *Only One Can Be Queen*, 16 inches, cloth. Photo by Robert Hirsch. Anne Wahl, *Anniversary Couple*, 10 inches, cloth. Photo by W. Donald Smith. Lisa Lichtenfels, *Desmond*, 25$^1/_2$ inches, mixed media. Photo by Lisa Lichtenfels.
Back Cover Photographs: Lynne Sward, *Goddess of Chocolate*, 16 inches, fabric, colored photo copies, bead and sequins. Ruth Landis, *Sewing Sisters*, each 18 inches, cloth. Photo by Ruth Landis. Maggie Iacono, *Marguerite*, 17 inches, felt. Photo by Jerry Anthony. Margi Hennen, *Turtle Woman...*, 9 inches, fabric. Photo by Warren Dodgson.
Title Page Photographs: Anne Mayer Meier, *Knobby-Kneed Bird Girl*, *Knobby-Kneed Flower Girl*, *Knobby-Kneed Fisher Girl*, each 16 inches, cloth. Photos by Jerry Anthony.

Attention Teachers: C&T Publishing, Inc. encourages you to use this book as a text for teaching. Contact us at 800-284-1114 or www.ctpub.com for more information about the C&T Teachers Program.

We take great care to ensure that the information included in this book is accurate and presented in good faith, but no warranty is provided nor results guaranteed. Since we have no control over the choice of materials or procedure used, neither the author nor C&T Publishing, Inc. shall have any liability to any person or entity with respect to any loss or damage caused directly or indirectly by the information contained in this book.

Trademarked (™) and Registered Trademarked (®) names are used throughout this book. Rather than use the symbols with every occurrence of a trademark and registered trademark name, we are using the names only in an editorial fashion and to the benefit of the owner, with no intention of infringement. Any mention of the use of paper clay by the author pertains to Creative Paperclay® products.

Library of Congress Cataloging-in-Publication Data
Oroyan, Susanna.
  Finishing the figure : doll costuming, embellishments, accessories/ Susanna Oroyan.
   p. cm.
  ISBN 1-57120-121-1
  1. Doll clothes. 2. Doll furniture. I. Title.
TT175.7 .O76 2001
745.592'2--dc21
                    00-011787

Published by C&T Publishing, Inc.
P.O. Box 1456
Lafayette, California 94549

Printed in Hong Kong
10 9 8 7 6 5 4 3 2 1

■ Robert Cunningham, *The Palace Musician at the Palace of Pearls*, 78 inches, Super Sculpey and wire armature. Photo by Pirak Studios, Ltd.

Thanks

A book does not happen in isolation.

This one, and the others before happened because…I had a grandfather who bought me left-handed scissors and encouraged me to sew a shirt….a grandmother who gave me a sewing basket and set the example of doing good work…a grandmother with a great imagination who told the most dramatic stories…a grandfather who loved books and would read anything aloud…a mother who let me sew by myself and never, ever discouraged me and a father who showed me how to use tools, let me work with his, then gave me my own. They showed me the basics, answered my questions, gave me the freedom to explore and experiment, and endured any number of my "creative messes."

When the messes evolved into the things we call dolls, I was fortunate to find fellow artists who taught their techniques and inspired me with their work.

When I wanted to tell how it was done, the same artists responded by sharing their work in photographs.

There was a publisher with foresight, and editors, working with detail, and design experts, who all took great care to refine my materials and make my ideas in words into books that we can hold in our hands.

And, as always, there is my husband Tom, who translates process into drawing with love and support.

My thanks to all…Susanna Oroyan

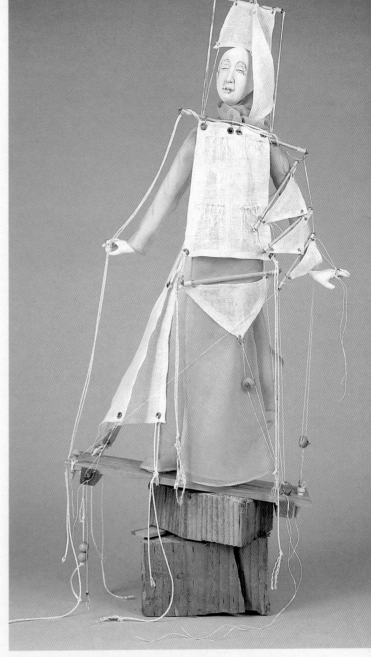

■ Susanna Oroyan, *The 93rd Empress — All A-hoo,* 20 inches, paper clay. Photo by W. Donald Smith.

Contents

■ Gretchen Lima, *Mother and Daughter,* 15 inches, cloth.
Photo by William Lemke.

■ Gretchen Lima, *Mother and Papoose,* 15 inches, cloth.
Photo by William Lemke.

■ Susanna Oroyan, *The Earthly Empress,* 20 inches, paper clay.
Photo by W. Donald Smith.

Preface

It All Depends...

Creating the figure and its character—whether sewn, sculpted, or assembled—is a major achievement. You take raw materials and put them together to make an "illustration of personality" or a statement about the human condition. However, there are many things that you can do and many things that you need to do before you can say, "Done."

Finishing the figure means dressing the doll, but only a few dolls are made to have removable clothes. Quite a few are pure form. The clothing you make might be removable or permanently applied, or you might just want to enhance the figure with surface embellishment, such as painting or embroidery. Dressed or not, finishing the figure also means creating its presentation, which can be anything from making accessories and settings to building support systems.

How can you put it all together? And how can you put it together with those extra touches that will make it a piece that will catch the viewer's eye and turn his head? It all depends on how you picture the finished figure. This means a lot of thinking. But you have already been thinking as you created the form of the character and considered its design. By the time you get to the finishing steps, you probably have a pretty good idea of how you want to end up.

If you see your ideas in sharp detail—as illustrations or little snapshots of life in the real, historical, or fantasy world—most likely you will be more interested in information about the construction of clothes and objects found in those worlds. Some of you will tend to have ideas where form or sculptural outline of the figure will be more important. Most likely you will be interested in surface design applications, such as beading, dyeing, and manipulating fabric.

Each and every thing you do for a figure, from shoe making to hair dressing to costume and furnishings, is a fully developed craft requiring years of study and practical experience to arrive at successful work. Doll makers also want to know it all now and have it available in one place.

But doll makers usually want to know at 2:00AM how shoe heels are constructed. Fortunately, doll makers usually only need to get a rough grasp of a concept or method. Once a doll maker has the basic idea, all sorts of wonderful, individual variations or necessary adjustments are made to solve any design problems. *Finishing the Figure* provides you with enough of the basic considerations in finishing a doll to get you started toward the particular solutions you might need. Take time to experiment and don't be afraid to waste time and materials. Not everything you do has to go on a finished piece.

Along the way, I add advice and insert some cautions. Take time to think about these comments as they are based on analysis of figures the best artists think are successful. Take a close look at the pages and pages of inspiring pictures. See if you can discover what special things the artists did to make their pieces "sing." When you finish a piece, you might have thoughts of shipping it off to an exhibit, starting a business or, at the very least, getting good photos for your own record-keeping and sharing. I'll talk about that, too.

As you read and study, remember that what you see here is just the tip of the iceberg. If I am successful, your head will be buzzing with new ideas and your hands trembling with anticipation. I hope you will use what you see to experiment, expand, and create new techniques of your own, and, in doing so, carry the tradition of doll making well into the 21st century.

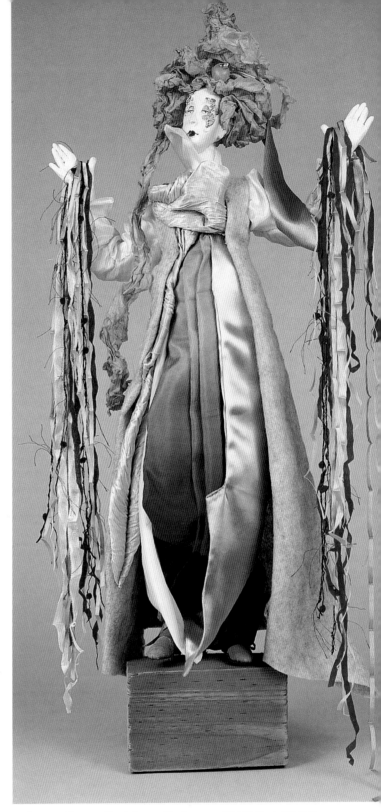

■ Susanna Oroyan, *The Inflammable Empress,* 20 inches, paper clay. Photo by W. Donald Smith.

■ Susanna Oroyan, *The Atmospheric Empress,* 20 inches, paper clay. Photo by W. Donald Smith.

Introduction

Costume and the Elements of Design

Before you grab the scissors and start cutting into that lovely expensive piece of fabric, you need to understand design.

Design consists of two major parts. One is the overall plan of what you want your figure to communicate. The other is the elements you consider when picking out directions and shapes to make that picture happen. You know the elements of design as form, line, proportion, color, texture, balance, scale, and motif.

By the time you get to "finishing," you have been working with the overall design for some time. The "Big Picture" is in your head. Some design elements have already been considered. For instance, you have already got a shape or form. That is the figure itself made to fit the type (realistic, abstract, or cartoon) you choose. Its line or body position is at least roughed in. You have also determined scale by the figure's size and proportion. Most likely you already have had some fairly definite thoughts about color and textures (types of fabric or applied materials). Now, the process will become one of refining, or sharpening the fuzzy edges of the Big Picture.

Four elements of design are very important in costume. They are line, scale, texture, and color. As you progress to completion, these elements take on a slightly more specialized meaning. The more settled parts, such as form and proportion, become the guides for specific decisions about each and every part that you add to the figure. In the end, however, all the elements will need to create a pleasant, harmonious relationship and reflect your personal style and point of view.

A Slightly Different Perspective

Line: *Accentuate the Positive*

The line of the figure or the body position you choose to accentuate becomes the base for your decisions. If you create a very curvy abstract piece, you will want to select finish treatments that emphasize rather than hide those round shapes. If you have a figure with bent knees or elbows, you will want to make sure those bone points are visible under even the most bulky costume. If a figure is seated in a chair, you want to consider how the outline of the chair reflects or enhances the line of the seated figure. In short, whatever else you do to your figure, all of it has to work "inside the line" you initially gave it.

Scale: A *World of Its Own*

In creating the form, you make decisions about its scale in relation to the general size of the figure and the relationship of its parts to the whole. Appropriate—not necessarily correct—scale is essential for any figure. Usually, we think of scale as having to do with relative sizes: X is too big for the doll or Y is too small for it. In finishing the figure, scale becomes equally important as we consider the relationship of sizes of things on the figure or in its background. This background should be thought of as the world the figure lives in. We might never see this world or any of its parts, but things that go with and on the figure need to look like they belong to that world.

The doll's world, or environment, is determined by the doll's materials, shape, detail, and scale. These may not be an accurate reflection of our real human world—or items you can find or buy. But anytime you make a doll or figure, you need to mentally project a background for it. This background needs to be in your mind when you work. You can think of it as a dollhouse, a landscape painting, or a theater stage, but visualize it clearly.

■ (Above) Sara Austin, *Angela* detail, 12 inches, cloth. Photo by Riviera Imaging.

■ Ima Naroditskaya, *From Cat's Life,* 8 inches, La Doll. Photo by Elena Polosukhina.

Realistic scale is probably the easiest to understand and the hardest to achieve. If you opt to create a realistic figure—one that looks as photographically human as possible—then the world of its accessories and background must reflect a miniaturized version of the real world. For instance, a male figure that is six inches tall lives in a world proportionately scaled to the world of a real six-foot man. If a chair seat in the real world is one-and-a-half feet from the ground, the chair seat in the figure's world will be one-and-a-half inches from the floor. If a leg on a real-world chair is two inches thick, then the leg of the miniature chair will be approximately an eighth-inch thick. Very small, indeed, but if you choose realism, then you have to do the math. Figure the size of the objects in accordance with the size of your figure and use your highly critical eye to get those details to be or appear to be exactly right.

Most dolls, however, are ever-so-slightly abstracted, exaggerated, or impressionistic. This allows the artist some leeway with scale and the rules will be the ones he makes. The important thing is that the combinations of materials work with the piece and enhance its expression. Or, if you choose to add a different note, use the part or item to underline or jolt the viewer purposefully.

Let's look at some examples:

■ You have made a doll with a fine, painted silk body. Would you use corduroy for its costume? Or would you try to find lightweight silky fabrics and fine laces?

■ You are making a costume of eyelet lace. Would you choose silk ribbon or grosgrain ribbon for trimming bows?

In the first case, you should reject the corduroy because its weight detracts and distracts from the delicacy of the silk figure. In the second case, the silk ribbon is too light and flimsy for the cotton eyelet.

The biggest problems in scale are the result of the temptation of materials. This is when you see some wonderful piece of fabric or trim and you try to force it into a costume just because you like it. There are some lovely metallic braids, but remember, on a doll most of them will be the scale of rope, not thread! A one-inch-wide band of sequin trim on your doll will be equivalent to a twelve-inch band in human scale. Each sequin would be the equivalent of four inches. Would you wear something that big? If you wouldn't, your doll won't either. You can still use the material, it just takes a bit of thinking about it. Take the braid apart. Sew several bands of sequins together and make a jacket for the doll or cut the bands into single or double strands. When you are tempted by a piece of material or trim, consider how many ways you can change it. Consider its potential rather than its current use.

■ Joyce Patterson, *Ann's Harley Spirit,* 17 inches, cloth. Photo by Joyce Patterson.

Another problem for a doll maker is finding a well-made, well-scaled accessory. We are always on the look-out for them. (And they do show up.) But are they really going to be the right blend with your piece?

At the beginning of my doll-making career, I found some wonderful letter openers. They were exquisitely detailed miniature Spanish swords with engraving and enamel detail. I bought four of them. In twenty-five years, I have only been able to make two dolls with the detail required in costume and sculpture to match them. Every time I thought I had a doll that would work, the sword was just too fine, too outstandingly different, so I ended up eliminating the sword idea and made something that did fit.

It's possible to find very accurately scaled and detailed toy bicycles typical of the 1940s. It's almost impossible for any doll maker to pass one up. To be used well, however, you have to think about it as a controlling factor in your doll design choice. First you measure the piece and determine the size of the doll that will fit. If it is four inches from the seat to the ground, you will need to make your doll no more than nine-inches tall. Not only will the doll have to be that size, it will have to be as near to photographically realistic as possible in order to not be overwhelmed by the bike's construction and detail. This means portrait sculpture. It means detail on clothing, such as topstitching on trousers, one-eighth-inch pleating, knitting on triple 0 needles, and fingers the size of toothpicks. Every single part of your doll and its costume must look like it lives in the same world as the bicycle. If these are not things you like to do or do well, then you ought to just enjoy the bike for itself. It's better not to force a figure into being just because you have a neat accessory.

■ Joyce Patterson, *Garage Sale Sally,* 17 inches, cloth.
Photo by Joyce Patterson.

Occasionally there are some exceptions. Joyce Patterson's *Ann's Harley Spirit* (page 9) is one and so is her *Garage Sale Sally.* The motorcycle character succeeds because the colorful and detailed machine creates a neat balance to the simple, light figure. The costume details are textural and white and befitting the abstract cloth figure. The same is true of *Garage Sale Sally.* The doll is no-bones-about-it stuffed cloth rather than painted realism. The garage-sale finds the doll carries are plastic or combined materials and not all in exact scale. How does this work? It works because the doll is truly an abstract, and it is made of material that doesn't resemble human skin. So, the doll itself creates its own world. Things that go in that world can also be non-human looking and non-human in scale.

Again, the consideration: do these things look like they could belong to this doll in her world? And the answer is yes, because this is an entirely made-up world. Even so, Joyce's selections were carefully made to fit that particular world.

As you can see, the entirely made-up world you create has to be a good piece of art. Like the doll, it must have a uniform design. A doll maker is an illustrator. Instead of showing you the doll in an entire setting, he might show you the doll and a portion of that setting.

Texture: *Filling Space*

Texture has to do with how the piece feels when you touch it—soft, smooth, rough, slick. It also involves what the eye tells the brain when it looks at the piece. When you decide what material your figure is to be made of, you make an initial decision about its texture. Every medium you use gives the piece a different visual feeling. A painted cloth figure will look and feel very different from a cloth figure of velour with embroidered features, or a felt figure with painted features. Painted porcelain looks and feels very different from glazed stoneware. In finishing the figure, you will choose items that will work with your basic surface.

And, equally important, you will design surfaces so that they make spaces and surfaces interesting to the viewer. I call this "filling in space" or "breaking up space." You might think of it as something similar to what a painter does when she puts small plants and shadows under trees. The idea is to give the viewer several things to touch imaginatively when she looks at the piece.

■ Jacqueline Casey, *Sweater Girl,* 12 inches, needle modeled from sweater.
Photo by Jacqueline Casey.

Usually problems happen when color and pattern take over and texture is left behind. But...but, you say, this doll *must* wear a solid blue dress. Or, you say, my figure just needs this floral print. Here is how using texture can let you have your cake and eat it, too.

Let's discuss the solid blue dress. The style is a very simple bodice and a full skirt—a style that could be 1860 or 1950 or "Alice in Wonderland." To keep the line and color, but make the dress more visually interesting, you'll need to provide a bit more detail in the basic construction.

Rather than plain gathers in the skirt and sleeves, precision cartridge pleats could be used. A contoured princess seam line could be used in the bodice. A roll of piping could be inserted between the bodice and the skirt. It's still a plain blue dress, but the eye has been given more to appreciate. What else? We could use a lighter or darker shade of the same blue to make a yoke for the bodice. We could take three or five rows of pin tucks along the lower edge of the skirt; we could add a pair of pockets...and it's still a plain blue dress. But we have broken up the space.

Color

A discussion of color in doll making is going to take more than a paragraph or two. No matter what shape or medium the figure is made of, color is often the most important consideration in finishing it. By the time you finish the basic figure, you've already made some color choices, selected skin tone (which might have been a multi-colored fabric), and perhaps a hair color. Now, as you add items or elements in the finishing, you will need to think about how you want the viewer to react to the figure and what colors it will need to reflect its world or time period. You are considering the psychology of color. Not only will the colors have to coordinate with the figure, but they will also need to project some emotional content. They will have to work well together without being overwhelming. In short, if some one says, "Wow, that is a big, red, angry doll" you want that reaction. If you didn't want that reaction, but that's what you got, then you need to re-assess your color choices.

■ Margery Cannon, *Red Riding Hood,* 18 inches, cloth.
Photo by Jan Schou.

■ Genie Geer, *Sascha,* 16 inches, cloth.
Photo by Anne-Marie Brombal.

■ Jane M. Carlson, *Poppy,* 27 inches, needle sculpture.
Photo by Ken Carlson.

Commercial Color Realities

Have we always had all of the colors? No. Even as you read this, chemists are developing new colors. Most of us have a good feel for what we need; the problem is that we can't find it. The design industry—fashion, furnishing, household accessories, and automotive, have color experts who get together and decide what will be "in" for the next year or two. This is done so that the various industries can coordinate their planning and so you can buy bath towels or bedspreads, paint, wallpaper, and toilet fixtures that will work together. For your doll making, an awareness of color-market trends means that you need to buy colors every few years so that you can have the color you need when it is out-of-style. The year you need dusty blue satin for a doll will surely be the year that bright blue is "in."

For costuming your historical figures, you need to become familiar with the era or part of the world you want to portray. You need to know what materials they had access to, and what vegetable or mineral materials might have been available for dyeing. Also what might have been common, or what was an expensive import. For example, natural wool and linen might have prevailed in ancient Rome. Yellow and green might have been the most common vegetable dyes. Red dye came from rust/iron. Where did imperial purple come from? It was an expensive Eastern import and as such only seen on very high-ranking people. So, be aware of the fashionable colors of an era.

Color Psychology

Color—and its absence—creates the mood of a doll, underlines the personality, and brings the strongest emotional response in a viewer. An understanding of color and the ability to use it effectively is of prime importance for the doll maker.

This is a serious and scientific subject that in full treatment takes volumes, and those works would be found under the several headings of physics, chemistry, psychology, and anatomy. Basically, working with color involves the properties of waves, refraction and absorption, the chemistry of pigments and dyes, how the mind works to perceive physically and culturally, as well as the actual function of the eye mechanism. Most of us live with color, respond to it, and use it on a daily basis. Sometimes, we are naturally good at working with color, sometimes we just take it a little too much for granted, and sometimes we are plain scared of it. My job here is to make you think about it seriously and be able to use it for your figure making.

Color is the result of light from the sun being broken into different wavelengths by the earth's atmosphere. So, amounts and types of light are going to be important factors in color use.

Color Theory: *A Little Lingo*

Colors are properties of light as it is broken by a spectrum. These are also called hues. Black is not a color, it is the presence of all color or the absence of light. White is not a color, it is unbroken light.

Hues are primary colors (intense), which cannot be produced by mixing any other colors together. Secondary colors are produced by mixing two primary colors together. Intermediate colors, the mixtures of primary and secondary, are colors that appear next to each other on a color wheel (primary red + secondary purple = red/violet).

All of the colors/hues can be made into tints by adding white or into shades by adding black. Tints and shades are referred to as values. The closer to white the lighter the value. The closer the hues are to the twelve primary, secondary, and intermediate colors, the more intense they are. Adding white or black to colors to create shades or tints reduces intensity.

First Step: *Working with Skin Tone*

No matter what is the body medium, its color will be the skin tone of your figure. Even if not much of the flesh is going to show, it will become the basis for your other color selections. Why? Because the viewer has a body himself, knows about bodies, and will automatically be able to project a whole flesh-covered body under surface additions. Humans have skin tones ranging from deepest dark-brown to almost white. Depending on the color of the sculpting medium or the color of the paints you use or mix to use on your dolls, they will have a skin tone with either a bluish or yellowish look. The first step in determining color for your piece is to know its skin tone.

■ Nancy J. Laverick, *Mozart,*
14 inches, cloth.
Photo by Nancy J. Laverick.

Skin Tones

Most doll makers use commercially available fabrics, flesh-tone paints, or pre-tinted sculpting media. Most craft paint and pen manufacturers have at least two or three flesh-tone colors. Usually, these provide a choice of a yellowish, blue/pink, or brown/red base. Colors mixed with yellow-orange will be complementary to blues and violets. Colors mixed with Cadmium red light will be complementary with yellow-green. And colors mixed with cadmium red medium will be complementary to blue-green. So, strange as this might seem, if the flesh has a yellow tint, then the figure will look best in cool colors, and if it has a red tint, it will look best in warm colors.

Do note that there is great variation of tone possibilities for each racial or ethnic group. You can't make generalizations based on hair color—such as blondes look good in pink. A better distinction is that some blondes look good in shell pink and some look good in rose pink. For the artist this means that any race can wear any color provided the base tone is complementary to the colors that the artist wants to use. Also be aware that flesh tones, since they are mixed by adding white or black, are less intense. This means you must be very careful in choosing your other colors so that their intensity does not threaten to overwhelm the figure's skin tone.

Color draping had a little zip of popularity a few years ago. Everyone was having it done and carrying around swatches of "their colors." Today, you might find a beauty consultant, make-up specialist, or beauty shop that can do it for you. Give it a try, it's very illuminating. If the color works with your skin, you will appear to be bright, almost lit up; if it doesn't, you will appear murky and tired looking. What is happening here is that you really are lighting up because those colors are complementary—they reflect different sides of the color wheel. Your doll has to wear its colors. Color draping can be used to determine your doll's color needs.

Color Psychology: *Important to Consider*

Very important: the colors you like might not be good for the doll or its intended message. (This is not "pop" pysch, clinical tests in academic laboratories have pretty much borne out what we generally accept.) Here is a summary list of color responses outlined by Faber Baron in his book *Color and Human Response*: I would like to interject that artists are most likely to respond to the question, What is your favorite color? with the question: What for?—meaning, I have favorite colors for various applications.

Baron outlines how we associate colors with personality and how our color preferences might reflect our own personalities as follows:

RED — impulsive, athletic, sexy, quick to make a judgment

PINK — youth, tenderness, affection

ORANGE — cheerful, friendly, luminous

YELLOW — innovation, originality, wisdom

YELLOW-GREEN — perceptive, perhaps timid

GREEN — nature, balance, normality, adjusted, civilized, conventional, overweight

BLUE-GREEN — charming, eccentric, sensitive, refined, fussy

BLUE — conservatism, accomplishment, devotion, introspection, cautious

PURPLE-VIOLET — sensitive, tasteful, high ideals, lover of arts

BROWN — homespun, sturdy, reliable, shrewd, sense of duty and responsibility

WHITE — emotionless, sterile, security, sobriety

BLACK — sophistication, death, despair

Whoo! I like them all. I am an artist and I can use them all.

Here's a thought: *If you are going to sell your work, color is going to attract the buyer. Maybe you don't like red, but the impulsive buyer might. Maybe you don't like purple, but the art collector might.*

■ Valerie Garber, *God's Fool,* 5 inches, wax over resin. Photo by Ken Worrow.

Color: *The Viewer's Expectation*

We tend to think in terms of "baby boys wear blue and baby girls wear pink." This is an adult Western-cultural perspective. We grown-ups tend to think of babies as fragile and soft, hence pale colors. If the baby had his or her choice, it would probably pick yellow or red because these are the colors that a baby will watch, reach for, or respond to. Therefore, the cultural response is an important factor. If making dolls for your baby to play with, pick from the primary and secondary basic colors. For adult collectors, have fun with pastels.

Here are some additional color associations based on intensity:

Hot

RED — blood, war, aggression, sex, Christmas

ORANGE — Halloween, fall

YELLOW — sun, warmth, cheerful, childlike

Cool

GREEN — peace

BLUE — bravery, loyalty, truth, clarity

PURPLE — royalty, elegance

PINK — tenderness, romance

BLACK — death

WHITE — purity

So, the colors you might choose for a soldier would be red and blue. The colors you choose for a pretty teenage girl might be pink or light blue. Or if you want to deliver a different message, what does a figure in a yellow uniform give? Perhaps a comic opera character? Can you make a sexy lady and pull it off in yellow?

Color and Light

Next consider light—just lighting. Do you work in daylight or artificial light? Is the artificial light fluorescent or tungsten? Colors will appear different in each type. For several years, the National Institute of American Doll artists held their annual exhibit in a hotel ballroom with very generalized, very distant tungsten lighting. The exhibits looked fine, but the year that gallery spotlights were brought in, the dolls became much punchier and we were amazed at what we had done. Good lighting in a photo or an exhibit venue will always make your piece look its best. As we work, we need to be aware that what we make in daylight will change color at night under work light. You need to test paints and fabrics in both as you work on a piece. I noticed that pieces I painted in the daylight were always much lighter and softer than those painted in artificial light in the evening. The lower intensity of the interior light made me paint in more color so I could see it. (You might want to invest in a specially made lamp that shows true color.)

So, before even starting to look at color selections, you need to consider: your preferences, your doll's skin tone, the audience you aim for, the message you want to achieve, the light you work in, and the light you want it to be seen in.

Color Design Elements and Considerations

Contrast is basically the difference in value against a background. For instance, red will have a high degree of contrast or be the dominant color against a white or light ground, but not against a black or dark background.

Balance for the figure maker comes into play when you have two or three colors close in value (amount of lightness or darkness). When you use such colors together as your main choices in equal amounts, neither will register strongly and the result can negate successful color impact in the piece. You can do it, but the choice needs to be a thoughtful, reasoned one with regard to the mood and impact you wish to communicate.

Scale in color refers to the intensity or the value of the hue. The impact or intensity of the color may be too big for the piece. The more intense (less tinted or shaded) a hue/color is the brighter it looks, and bright looks big and bold. If you imagine a person wearing a true red blouse, you would call that loud, bright, bold, or hot. Suppose you want your doll to wear a primary red. The doll is one-fourth the size of the human so the color needs to be reduced in intensity by tinting or shading. That will make it appear to wear a primary red, but the color will not overwhelm the viewer or the other parts of the figure. The color then will be right for the scale of the figure. It is very necessary to be aware of color intensity when you pick colors for your realistic human figures. It is less necessary for abstract and play types that might have exaggerated body and face treatments. Often when a figure seems "wrong" the problem might be that the color is off-scale.

Also, notice how realistic figures made by more successful artists typically use colors of lower intensity and how often even those colors rarely show up in large expanses. The color-conscious artist will use trim or embellishments to break up large single-color areas to lower the color intensity and make the piece itself more important than its colors. Really careful artists, especially those working with figures of fifteen inches or less, will tea-dye or otherwise treat even further to lower the intensity of small-scale prints and solids. Remember, even small-scale prints, such as those quilters work with, are made for humans and quilts—they are too big and bright for dolls.

Bright colors in prints, polka dots, checks, and stripes can be used very effectively in spite of their intensity. The main issue is that the body, hair, and facial colors will need to be kept equally intense. In this case, think "clown" and remember that in most cases when a real human wears patterns in bold, bright colors, they wear face make-up or masks to enhance a funny, happy, bouncy image.

The first step toward using intense, large-scale colors is to carefully plan your sculpture. It probably should be exaggerated or abstract in form. In either clay or cloth that means a more cartooned face. The face itself should have some bright highlighting, such as bright pink cheeks, very red lips, or dark, arched eyebrows. Its facial expression should be dramatic. We might expect the feet to be fat or flat and somewhat clunky/chunky in look. The hands might be a fat, abstract shape, and might not have fingers. When we have a good body form going, then we can add the brightness—carefully. If we want the face to register, we don't want anything busily distracting around it. This means that we might use a pattern of bold solid red and white squares for a body, but we would take darker values of blue, perhaps with a small patterned print, and vary them in patterns with striping or quilting to make them appear smaller than the facial features, to make a vest or collar and hat. The darker solids allow the viewer to register the character in the face—and not just a splashy bunch of colors—by creating a frame around it. Carrying out a theme of primary colors, the hat might have a yellow flower. A small print used in the vest might have a little hint of the secondary colors, orange and purple, as well as some yellow. Does this mean bright colors can only be used on clowns or abstracts? No. For more refined figures, such as a real person in a Latin American dance costume, you use the colors in much smaller pieces, perhaps offset with white, and continually check placement so that the body doesn't disappear in a riot of glorious color.

Be Sneaky with Color

Colors are often chosen because cultural associations just seem to make them right. For instance, if you were to do a bride in the traditional contemporary white, you could end up with a big sea of lightness. The reverse is true for a Victorian widow in black. There are some ways to make these problems work out with sneaky effects. For instance, you might vary your bridal white by combining white fabrics with varying intensities of yellow (ivory). You might shade the inside of pleats and gathers; you might put one shade of white on top of a train and another underneath. The widow might be given color interest by adding gray, lavender, and purple accents. The inside of her bonnet might show a very dark-purple lining, her handkerchief might have a lavender border, and her black velvet purse might be embellished with black braid or jet beads. Of course, there are some times when unrelieved areas will add to the impact. On my *Dollmaker* '96 figure, I purposely made the figure very pale and her dress deep dull, black velour. Why? Because if I put the figure on a black background, the viewer's eye would be focused immediately on what the head wore and the hands were doing. The figure had to have a dress, but this way, the dress in no way detracted from the action.

■ Colleen Ehle Patell, *O' Bellagio*, 25 inches, cloth over wire armature. Photo by Peter N. Fox.

Other Color Considerations: *Local and Historical Color*

When fabrics were mainly homemade, coloring materials used were locally found. Think about it. In the illustrated manuscripts of the middle ages, we see peasants wearing variations of brown, mustardy yellow and greens...naturally found vegetable dye colors. Blues came from indigo or woad. Until the end of the Renaissance in Europe, very intense reds, blues and greens are seen being worn by more well-off people who could afford to buy their cloth already dyed. Rusty reds and blacks came from mineral dyes such as iron. Even though there was a fairly healthy business in producing colored fabric in the Middle Ages, we don't see many other colors in European art until the increase in international trade and urban living that happened in the 16th and 17th centuries.

At that point, we see colors such as pink, rose, teal, and steel. So it went until the 1850s when aniline dyes brought in the extremely sharp colors of magenta, turquoise, lime green, and chrome yellow. Imagine a world in which these colors rarely appeared in nature and never appeared in cloth. As a doll maker choosing colors, you will help your figure by using colors that reflect its historical period and place.

A Little More To It

The element of problem solving always enters into the design of a figure. Two of the most challenging and difficult areas to deal with are the best way to use actual historical fashions and how to use but not abuse inspirational material. Let's have a look.

The Historical Element

Some will choose to make very accurate portrait figures with clothing that is typical of a specific historical era. Some will pick and choose style details from various eras to use on their own very unique figures. Either way, you might want to consider the following when you design your finishing steps.

Picking Your Presentation

When you study costume sources, you might find several variations of design shown for one era or style. You might decide to do a figure in a full hoop skirt. This could be a single solid or patterned fabric gathered to the waist. Maybe the skirt is shown with a band of lace running around it. Another illustration might show a figure with a skirt of tiered ruffled fabric detailed with tiny rosebud and ribbon nosegays. Another might show a plaid fabric sewn in diagonal bands. The second design, although much more difficult to reproduce, will be the most effective because it is the more inter-

esting to the viewer. The third design of the plaid would be very authentic of the taste of the era, but it is not the image most usually accepted by the contemporary viewer.

Authenticity

We all know that the film industry has shown us idealized versions of historical costume. Compare a neatly corseted film pioneer heroine in pastel calico with actual photos of the pioneers. In early photos you will notice that working women wore loose sack dresses which were made of heavyweight fabrics, did not have lacy trims or even ruffles, and were often rumpled and dusty. When you make decisions about historical costume, give a thought to the image you want to portray and how that might align with the fact that clothing was not laundered, certainly not perma-press, and often very difficult to iron. Give a thought to the fact that working-class people probably had only two or three sets of clothing. Think about how clothing functioned. In the 1600s, for instance, a lady might dress up by changing her sleeves from plain to fancy, or by changing her petticoat. Did you ever wonder how ladies kept their long skirts clean? They had dust ruffles. My grandmother told of taking these ruffles off, cleaning them and sewing them back on again—because the dresses were only spot-cleaned and not laundered that often. But can you imagine taking off and sewing on five yards of ruffles as part of your laundry work? Do you suppose the ordinary housewife with no servants took the time to press these ruffles with a flat iron?

Cuts: *Cause and Effect*

The expression "clothes make the man" is not far off the mark. The way a costume is constructed will make a person assume a particular posture or move in certain ways. In costuming and posing figures, especially ones done in historical costume, it is extremely important to keep this in mind if you want to add the finishing touch of authenticity to your piece. For instance, the girdle, very high heels, and very narrow sheath skirts of the 1950s made women walk in shorter, almost mincing steps with toes pointed out. The skintight clothing or very loose clothing currently worn allows a loping slouching look. The tight cut of 18th century women's bodices over corsets that ended below the waist in front and the similarly tight cuts of gentlemen's coats of the same era were purposefully made to create a graceful, sinuous movement or look. When Madame Pompadour reclines for her portrait it is because her clothes did not allow her to sit up straight. Never forget the cut of the pattern creates the "line and look" of an era.

Mix and Match

The idea of "separates" is not a new concept in fashion. In fact, until about 1900, the one-piece costume was usually a sack, chemise, or morning gown which was considered "undress." What you see in a fashion drawing or portrait painting that looks like one garment is probably a combination of several interchangeable parts. Typically, from the time America was discovered until World War I, a woman's wardrobe consisted of chemise, petticoats, corset, skirt, bodice and often pairs of sleeves and assorted collars. (Underwear as we know it was not commonly worn until the early 1800s.) The garment closest to the body was the short-sleeved (nightgown-appearing) chemise. Over that went the petticoat and over that went a skirt which was sometimes split at the front to show off fancywork on the petticoat. Corsets were laced up the front (or back if you had a maid) and were sometimes covered with decorative stomachers. The bodice, a separate jacket or vest-like construction, was pinned, tied, or laced up over the corset. Plain or decorative sleeves sometimes could be tacked in as desired. Bustles, panniers, bum-rolls, and other padding were tied or tacked on over the petticoats as current fashion shapes demanded. For daily work, a housewife could wear her everyday petticoat and corset over her chemise, but for dress, she could add a fancy petticoat, tack a pair of lacy sleeves onto her corset, then cover it with a stomacher and tie on a lace collar. In costuming historical figures, you do not have to make all these separate pieces, but you should create the costume to look like it was composed that way.

Working With Inspiration

There isn't a one of us who hasn't seen a photo or drawing that just shouted "Make me as a doll!" Many artists get their inspiration from the work of graphic artists whose rendering is highly suggestive of specific fabric designs and texture. But we can't make direct copies just because we like something. Copying is infringing copyright. Any time you want to make a copy of another's original art or even make a portrait of a living person, you need to get written permission to do so from the owner of the image. It might take a little work, but more often than not, you can get the permission.

Better yet, don't copy exactly, use the other artist's work as learning material. Notice how she used colors, notice how she used textures. Notice how she treated form and type. And then, if you must, make a translation of some element of the work rather than the whole thing. Make the translation work with your design and become part of your expression.

Even if you do get permission to copy an image or a personality, it fails time after time because artists attempt to translate the elements exactly as suggested by the graphic artist's costume concept.

Reaction To The Key

Is all this scary? Sure it is. However, most of the artists whose work you see in this book—and some are beginners—were never frightened by the idea of "me" (my lack of skill, knowledge, my insecurities) costuming a doll. The key to it all is that they don't worry about themselves in this picture. They see the work as necessary to finishing the figure. Almost all will tell you that they had to do what they did because their initial idea, the figure and its character, required it. And they wanted to do it for the figure, wanted to do it bad enough to risk failure. They will tell you that they often weren't sure if something would work, but they tried it anyway just to see. Maybe they re-did it after they saw how they could do it better. They will groan and tell you it took a week and 18 tries to make a skirt drape in just the right way. They will tell you with pride that they made the effort to learn a craft—like beading or weaving—because the idea they had needed it. They will tell you with delight of things they had to invent because they couldn't find a method or a material that worked. All will tell you it takes work, persistence, failure, critique, problem solving, learning, experimentation, and time. But, above all, it takes starting. All you need is an idea and the will to make it happen.

■ Julie McCullough, *Cha Cha,* 24 inches, cloth. Photo by John Nollendorf.

■ elinor peace bailey's preliminary sketches for Chartreuse with coordinating fabric. The design challenge was to use printed fabrics provided. elinor's solution was to make the figure a solid, hot color and use the prints as subordinate costume elements. She made her own rules. They were different rules, but she was true to them and the result is a very unique piece. Photos by Isaac Bailey.

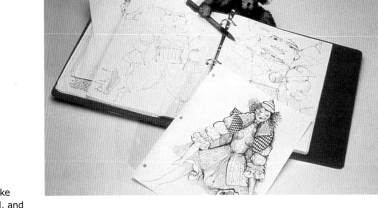

■ Susanna Oroyan, *Autumn Zephyr,* 24 inches, cloth. My solution to the same fabric challenge was to make the figure in white, use the colors as costume detail, and the print as the base. Another solution might have been to make the body of print and the costume of solids. Photo by W. Donald Smith.

■ elinor peace bailey, *Chartreuse,* 25 inches, cloth. Photo by Isaac Bailey.

■ Patti Medaris Culea, *A Tribute to Earl Davis,* 20 inches, cloth.
Photo by Bob Hirsch.

■ Lori Jett, *Fat Cat,*
24 inches, cloth, paper clay, mixed media.
Photo by Lori Jett.

■ Susanna Oroyan, *Granny Mulliner,* 18 inches, polymer clay.
Photo by W. Donald Smith.

CHAPTER ONE

Stuff and Stitches

A would-be doll maker once wrote to me saying that she would like to make the dolls shown in my book, but she couldn't find the materials. Her letter came from a fairly good-sized urban area, an area where I have several doll-making acquaintances who have lots of good stuff. Her priorities were backwards. She needed to let her idea, not the material someone else used, begin her doll. Once you have an idea, you search for the right stuff and there can be a lot of thrill and suspense in the hunt. Where could this material be? In a fabric store, thrift store, electrical supplier, hardware store, novelty shop? Will you find it? How can you save or change the idea to work with what you can find?

25 Boxes, 18 Drawers, 4 Bolts & 2 Bins

I make and design all kinds of dolls, from stuffed cloth to sculpted characters to rather far-out abstract constructions. I should have something of everything, but I have found there is a great deal I can do without and still make a good piece. Of course, you can't have too much, but you really do need to be a little selective about what types of stuff you need. Let me tell you what's in my stuff stash. Chances are if I don't have it, you might not need it either.

■ Two drawers are full of yarns and fibers, in all types of colors and textures. (Multi-ply yarns can be pulled apart to create new strings.)

■ Two drawers full of plastic boxes with beads — can't have too many beads; they can be used to make dolls themselves, their jewelry and accessories, as well as costume embellishments.

■ Two drawers full of ribbons, mostly one inch wide or less, mostly solid colors, metallic, or textured. Beware of old silk ribbon — it weakens and frays or tears when you try to work with it.

■ Four drawers of lace — mostly antique pieces. Some yardage of narrow cotton edgings

■ One drawer of old handkerchiefs

■ (Above) Susanna Oroyan, *First Doll* detail, 15 inches, cloth. Photo by W. Donald Smith.

■ One drawer of stockings, pantyhose, and tights (also works well as fairy fabric)

■ One drawer of acrylic paints, fabric pens, and assorted coloring stuff

■ One drawer of oil paints, brushes, and accessories for painting

■ One drawer of artificial flowers (from old hats)

■ One drawer of odd bits of embroidered lightweight fabrics

■ One drawer with a jar of buttons, and assorted cording, fringe and large trim (haven't used much of it)

I use photocopier paper boxes to store my stuff and this is what I have in them:

1. Box of Christmas novelties and accessories (I had two but got rid of excess)
2. Box of leather for shoes
3. Box of fur and wool scraps
4. Box of base materials and stands (I have another back-up box in the garage)
5. Box of mohair — wefted yardage, roving, some yarn for hair
6. Box of solid cottons, stripes, and patterns
7. Box of old small cotton prints, 1930s and 40s
8. Box of printed silks — mostly small prints and textures, ties and the like
9. Box of metallic fabrics – small scale
10. Box of lace – yardage or old clothing, eyelets, etc.
11. Box of velours
12. Box of velvets – just in case, also for covering bases
13. Box of knits – textured sweater bits and small scale patterns
14. Box of wool – small plaid, fine solids (hardly get into this box)
15. Box of filmy, glittery fabric – chiffons, silk organza, organdy
16. Box of hat materials – parts of old hats, feathers, flowers, wire
17. Box labeled "weird stuff," parts of old table runners, vintage clothes
18. Box of plain silk
19. Box of patterned silk
20. Box of textured silk and brocade

21. Box of white fabrics

22. Box of neutral fabrics

23. Box of odd stuff—wood scraps

24. Box of odd stuff—metal scrap, wire, hardware, springs, rods and tubes

25. Box of odd stuff—true junk, but you never know

Miscellaneous

Bin full of felt yardage and scraps—more than I need

Bin full of fabrics for clothes for me —someday!

Bolt of batiste

Bolt of lightweight muslin

Bolt of heavyweight muslin

Bolt of flesh-colored felt

And this does not count two cupboards and three drawers with sculpture and mold stuff, two sewing machines, and assorted tools and sewing basics. Notice that only about half the stash is fabric and a good amount of that is not purchased yardage.

I also have a considerable amount of vintage clothing. The rule here is that if it is interesting, different, and of museum quality, then that is where it belongs. Even badly damaged pieces of clothing can be restored for display. Give some thought to the costume heritage and educational value before getting the scissors. If a piece is really shot, or foxed, feel free to make salvageable pieces live again in a doll.

This is really far more than I need. If I made dolls every day for the rest of my life, I would never use it up. For the first 20 years I made do with about half that amount and still created well over 200 collector figures. The amount doubled a few years ago when I bought a considerable portion of a collector/maker's estate—too many rare and wonderful things to pass up, but I am passing them on all the time. Mostly, I kept a store of basic materials, only bought when I knew what I needed for a specific project, and tossed the scraps. Save your money and space for the really good stuff. Get rid of the scraps—if you used it once, you probably don't want to repeat it again. When I get an idea, I hope it's inspired by something I have or can create from what I have...and mostly I can. Even though when we want something, we want it immediately, it's a better idea to keep up your knowledge of local store stock, have a good file of source catalogs, and be prepared to wait for a mail order.

Lastly, there is nothing the matter with being a collector of fabrics and stuff. If it makes you happy, get it. However, don't make yourself frustrated because you feel obligated to do something with it. This makes you automatically and always behind. If you like to accumulate stuff, consider yourself its temporary caretaker and sometime user. Its life can go on someday with another collector/maker who will love it as much.

Sewing

You want to make figures, but you don't know how to sew. (Not surprising in this day when women work outside the home and children are clothed off the rack.) However, don't let that stop you. If you can thread a needle, you can sew well enough to begin to costume. For most of the costuming in this book, all that is required is to be able to put a needle into and out of fabric. Stitches can be of a type and placement that suit your design. It is just a matter of pushing the needle in and out of fabric to join two pieces together. Neatness only counts in so far as messy stitching areas should be hidden. You might find it easier and faster to sew straight seams on a sewing machine. Detailed instructions (and quite often lessons) come with sewing machine purchases. If you want to do it, you will. If you try simple approaches, pretty soon you will find yourself experimenting with the more complex.

If you have no experience in sewing your own clothing, you might find it beneficial to seek out and take a basic sewing class or two. If you learn better on your own, purchase a simple pattern and make it using inexpensive materials. At the least this will familiarize you with the basic sewing terms, cuts, and construction methods—and might result in new clothes for yourself. Along with sewing classes, try giving yourself a self-taught course through the sewing and tailoring books in your local library. You can always experiment with the various techniques using scrap materials. If you are just plain unhappy with a needle and thread, this will be your chance to be inventive with glue, wrappings, ties, and whatever surface embellishments you are willing to try. There is no rule that says costumes must be sewn or even that figures must be either sculpted or stitched. If you have ideas you want to make into figures, you will find a way to express them...and what you work out might give us a new way of looking at finishing the figure.

Basic hand-sewing stitches used in doll making:

- whip stitch or overcast stitch
- hemstitch
- ladder stitch
- basting stitch
- blind stitch
- blanket stitch

CHAPTER TWO

Pattern Drafting

Every original doll is going to require original costuming. Sometimes this can be very frightening. Naked dolls have nice form, painted dolls are interesting, but there might come a day when you need to construct realistic clothing to make your figure be who it wants to be.

Older doll makers who learned to sew by making their own clothes and those who come to doll making from a fashion background are often familiar with the shapes of clothing patterns and the methods of making them fit. In this day of "off-the-rack" clothing, younger people just never have had the sewing experiences. Where and how to begin is all a mystery. And there is no one set of steps I can outline for perfect results.

Most libraries will have anywhere from a few to several books on costume and many will show the pattern shapes that result in specific looks. Later in Chapter 4, I show many of the basic shapes, but for every one I show, there are probably six more that you can find in other books.

There are two ways to costume design. The first is flat pattern drafting. This is essentially drafting out the shapes with pencil, paper, compass, and curved templates or sketching the shapes free hand, using a tape measure to reference your constructed body. The second, discussed in the next chapter, is called draped pattern making. It requires a firm form—your doll body—which is draped with fabric. The fabric is pinched up and pinned to the shape of the hard form and then excess fabric is cut away. The costume can be constructed directly on the body and a paper pattern might not even be needed. Once you get the hang of it, you will find it fast and easy. This is the way I do costuming for my dolls.

In brief, the differences are:

Flat Pattern Drafting — measuring, drawing, paper pattern, muslin test pieces, machine sewn, removable clothing, sometimes bulky

Draped Pattern Making — final clothing, paper pattern optional, best fit, 80 percent handsewn, usually not removable

For those mainly interested in costuming uniform bodies such as porcelain reproductions and toy-like play dolls, there are several good books containing both ready-to-use patterns and step-by-step instructions.

Whichever way you ultimately decide is best for you, you need to remember that doll costuming is not exactly the same as making full-sized human clothing. The difference lies in scale. In most cases you want to make the human costume, but the fabric will be too heavy.

■ (Above) Karan Schneider, *Bavarian Santa* detail, 21 inches, Premo. Photo by Studio Rossi.

■ Nancy Cronin, *The Maid*, 18 inches, Super Sculpey. Photo by Nancy Cronin.

■ Bob Doucette and Tom Slotten; *Sorry, Wrong Room*; 21 inches, paper clay. Photo by Cusene Photography, Larry Estrin.

Pattern Drafting

Example 1: Flat Pattern to Form Fit — *Santa*

Here, we have a sculpted figure ready to be dressed in a traditional Santa costume. Notice the form has been padded so that a belt will fit around the top of the hip and beneath the tummy and that the upper thigh has been given a bit more thickness. You will also want to remember that the bone "corners" such as shoulders, hips, knees, elbows and ankles will have little or no "fat" over them even on a very heavy-set figure. We always want to begin with the correct anatomical shape. The idea is to fit the body, not stuff the clothing, or hang it on an assembly of sticks.

This figure illustrates a stuffed body form made with little or no reference to actual human anatomy. It would be difficult, if not impossible, to make clothing look realistic on this body. This shape dictates an abstract or cartooned look in clothing as seen in the work of Calhoun, McCullough, and Feroy.

This figure, built on a framework of dowels inserted into a wood base lacks muscle structure or body padding. Without it, the clothing will hang awkwardly. The work entailed to make it look realistic will be frustrating and time consuming. It is much faster and more satisfying to begin with a good form.

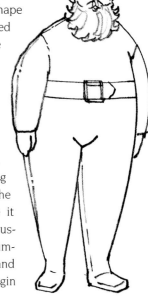

■ Lynne Calhoun and Debbi McCullough, *Father-in-law,* 15 inches, cloth, no armature. Photo by Lynne Calhoun.

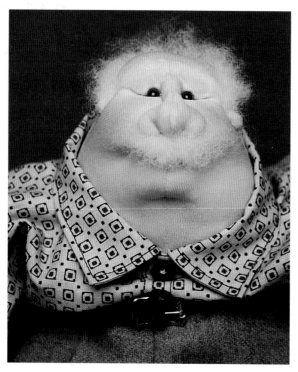

■ Meo Feroy, *Funky Fred,* 15 inches, polyester knit. Photo by Meo Feroy.

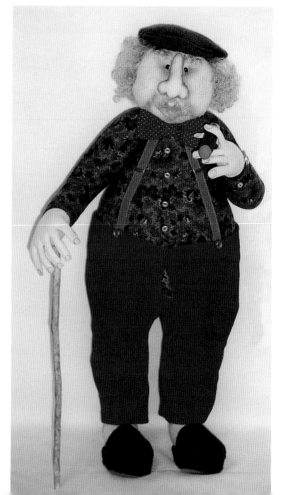

Measuring and Setting Drawing Points

Measuring

1

To make a flat pattern for a jacket side front that will fit the illustrated figure, begin with a large piece of paper, a tape measure, and a pencil.

2

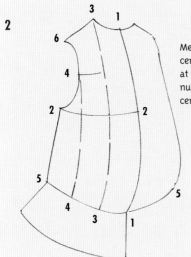

Measure points (5 to 5) from center of side to center of side at waist (belt level). Divide number in half to determine center front (point 1).

Next measure the center front from neck to waist (points 1 to 1). Then measure from the underarm center to the front (points 2 to 2). Measure points 3 to 3 from neck to waist.

3

Drafting

Use your pencil to make a light mark directly in the body fabric. Points 3-3 should be parallel to points 1-1. Draw points 3-3 on your paper. On paper, draw points 1-1 and 2-2 at right angles (90 degrees) to each other. On the doll body, locate the point of the arm curve closest to the center (point 4 above). Measure 4-4 and draw the line 4-4. On paper it will be parallell to points 1-1 and 3-3. Measure and draw the line 5-5 (it will not be parallel to 2-2 if tummy is fat at waist side). Measure and draw the line 3-6 from neck to shoulder top. You have now set the points of the pattern.

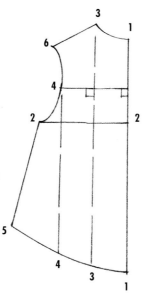

Use a curve to draw the arm hole opening from points 6-2 and the lower edge from points 5-1. The result is your basic pattern shape. You might wish to cut this shape in fabric and lay it on the figure to check for accuracy. If not exact, trim cloth and paper pieces until they match the form. Note that because the waistline is curved, the fabric test piece might not lie exactly smooth at the waistline. When sewing, this difference is eased in to fit the shape of the curve with a gathering stitch.

Judith Klawitter, *Old World St. Nicholas,* Super Sculpey. Photo by Mark Bryant.

Barbara Chapman, *Father Christmas,* 31 inches, paper clay. Photo by Bob Hirsch.

Drawing the Paper Pattern

1

First trace your paper pattern on another piece of paper. Determine how much of an overlap you want to show on the jacket front. Add this to the center line I–I. This becomes the facing fold line (A–A).

2

Flip the paper shape along the fold line and trace the outline of the neck and a portion of the shoulder line as shown.

3

Decide how wide the facing will be at the bottom of the jacket (on an 18-inch figure this might be about $1/2$ inch).

4

Use the curve to draw the line from the shoulder facing to the hem (waistline) as shown. The outline shape you have now contains the basic sewing lines. You need to add $1/4$ inch all around to arrive at the cutting line.

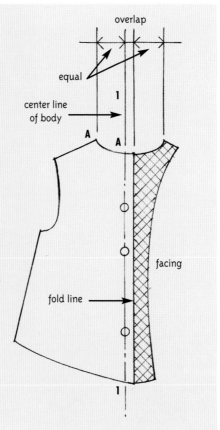

On most patterns the dashed line is the sewing line and the solid line is the line followed for cutting out the fabric. So, the solid measurement lines you started with in drafting the shape become the dashed sewing line.

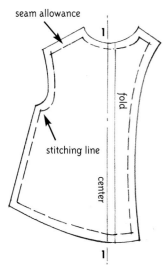

■ Helen L. Langhorne, *Santa is Legendary*, 12 inches, polymer clay, wire armature. Photo by Taylor Dabney.

Jacket

1

Gathered Skirt

Santa's jacket has a sewn-on skirt. To construct a flat pattern for this piece, measure around the waist, and multiply the measurement by $2^1/2$. Hem this piece on each end, then gather to fit the constructed jacket bottom to the fold line. Fold the facing back over the gathered piece and the right side of jacket bottom, and sew. After sewing, trim the corners and turn the facing to the inside.

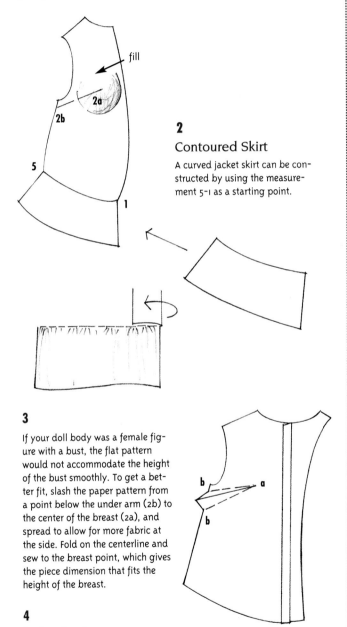

fill

2a
2b
5
1

2

Contoured Skirt

A curved jacket skirt can be constructed by using the measurement 5-1 as a starting point.

3

If your doll body was a female figure with a bust, the flat pattern would not accommodate the height of the bust smoothly. To get a better fit, slash the paper pattern from a point below the under arm (2b) to the center of the breast (2a), and spread to allow for more fabric at the side. Fold on the centerline and sew to the breast point, which gives the piece dimension that fits the height of the breast.

b
a
b

4

Jacket back

Construct the back using the same measurement points as the front. The center back line from neck to waist may be cut on the fold if you ease the waistline with gathers. If a center seam is desired, do not forget to add a seam allowance.

1

Measure line 1-1 around the maximum width of the hand/thumb on a sculpted hand. (A soft bendable hand can have a slightly narrower sleeve). Then, measure and draw the line 2-2 at the underarm. Next, measure and draw the line 3-3 from top of hand to top of shoulder. Use ruler and measurements to set points on paper. Use the curve to draw the sleeve cap.

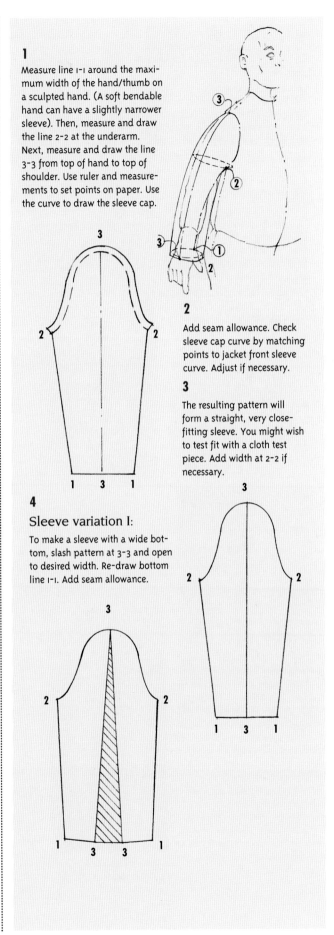

2

Add seam allowance. Check sleeve cap curve by matching points to jacket front sleeve curve. Adjust if necessary.

3

The resulting pattern will form a straight, very close-fitting sleeve. You might wish to test fit with a cloth test piece. Add width at 2-2 if necessary.

4

Sleeve variation I:

To make a sleeve with a wide bottom, slash pattern at 3-3 and open to desired width. Re-draw bottom line 1-1. Add seam allowance.

Flat pattern drafting may look very mechanical and exact; however, it is always best to cut and sew a muslin test piece (designers call this a toile) to check that the pieces will do what you want them to do in final shaping.

More complex pattern pieces can be drafted from the basic jacket, sleeves and trousers shown here by enlarging and reducing slashes in the basic shapes. See specific sections for variation in cuts for different styles and added parts, such as collars and cuffs.

Sleeve variation II:

To make a sleeve wider at the top, slash pattern 3-3, 3-4, and 3-5 so you have four pieces. Fan the pieces so that the bottom matches the narrow wrist measurement 1-1 and the top spreads as desired. Use a curve to re-draw sleeve cap line. Re-check measurement of lines 2-1 and re-draw pattern bottom.

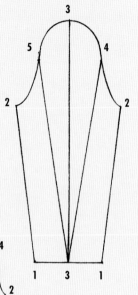

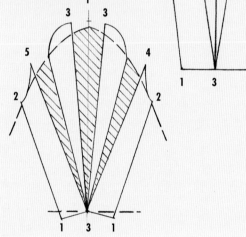

■ Karan Schneider, *Bavarian Santa,* 21 inches, Premo. Photo by Studio Rossi.

Trousers

Trousers for Santa are constructed in the same method using measurements as shown. Begin with side leg measurement 1-1. Measurement 2-2 is from the side of the leg to the center of the crotch and it is at right angle to line 1-1. Measurement 2-3 is from the center crotch to the lower leg. 1-4 is from the side of the hip to the center front. This measurement will be slightly less than 2-2 on the leg. Measure 4-2. Draw the curve (right) from 4-2. Remember sewing is done with the right sides of the fabric inside. When the curve is sewn and the fabric turned to the right side, the curve will reverse to fit the bulgy lower tummy.

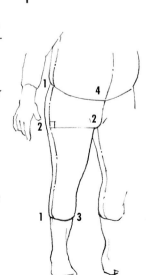

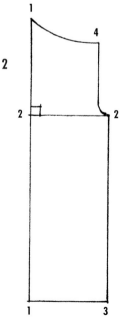

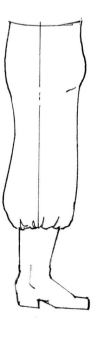

Determine desired length 1-1 — a little longer than finished length if you want to make the fabric gather at the boot top. Add seam allowances. Repeat drafting process for trouser back pattern if body back is shaped differently. Two pattern pieces are cut and sewn at the waist to crotch line 4-2 to make the front, two for the back. The back and front are laid together and the side seams 1-1 are sewn; then, the inside seam is sewn 3-2-3.

CHAPTER THREE

Applied Costume

As opposed to the measuring and drafting of flat pattern making, applied costuming works directly with fitting fabric to the doll, tucking it, and trimming it to the form. When the draped piece is shaped in the actual costume fabric, it can be sewn and attached without making a paper pattern. Or, the draped fabric piece can be used to draw a paper pattern. Most artists making one-of-a-kind figures use some variation of the draped method. Although it takes more words to describe, it takes much less time to do as most of the costume is cut and sewn right on the figure.

Some General Guidelines to Costume

In doll making, we use the draped method in all parts of costuming from shoes to headgear. The resulting figure is not a body with clothes put on, it is rather a collage of fabric, trim, and accessories. To illustrate the draped method, I am going walk you through the basic steps I used in costuming two of my character figures in period clothing. While it is not possible to give you step-by-step instructions in this format, I hope the overview will provide you the confidence you need to explore further on your own.

For any figure costume there are four important rules:

RULE 1 Reduce bulk. Trim/grade all seam allowances. Use press cloth and steam iron to press at every stage. Pound the iron on the fabric to shrink/mash fibers into desired shape. Pockets and collars can be "glued together" by inserting a tiny bit of fusible interfacing between layers so that they lie flatter. Hand sew or glue on trimmings. Machine stitching trim makes fabric bulk up, is visible and out of scale, and shortening stitch length makes seams harder. On the other hand, machine topstitching and some machine pattern stitches are often better scaled to dolls than applied trims. Use your machine pattern stitches to create your own brocaded or bordered fabrics.

RULE 2 Work from the inside out.

RULE 3 Don't do it if you don't have to.

RULE 4 Finish all parts that a person could see including underskirts. This might mean hemming and making French seams.

Costume 1 *The Opera Singer*

The major part of any costume is the idea or operating concept. Some like to sketch this. I usually begin with a general idea of the costume shape or era. In the examples, the ideas are an 18th century gentleman and an Edwardian lady both in formal costume. Equally important is the individual character's biography or "story." I have to have a very good idea of who they are and what they would do and wear before I begin. Any changes or adjustments to the costume design—and there will be some—are based on the original concept of character. It's similar to gift shopping when you say, "Oh, Jane would never wear that orange sweater" or "Grandma just loves rhinestone jewelry." Your doll persona has to "live" in your mind in order to make him "speak" to your viewer. Sometimes that message has to be sharp and detailed, and sometimes it just has to be able to suggest a thought or question in the viewer's mind.

■ (Above) Susanna Oroyan, *The Opera Singer* detail, 18 inches, cloth. Photo by W. Donald Smith.

■ Susanna Oroyan, *Minerva Mulliner,* 19 inches, cloth. Photo by W. Donald Smith.

Several years ago, I made two different sculpted character heads and molds for each. After making four of these characters as fairly diverse people, I began to think that since they looked alike, they must be related. I decided they were members of two related families of British eccentrics—the Mulliners and the Forbes—and I started making up an elaborate story to connect them into a family tree that stretched back into the mists of history. A few more figures and pretty soon friends and collectors were playing the game and suggesting character ideas to me to make and fit into the story. Over the course of several years nearly 60 members were made.

The *Opera Singer* is one of my Mulliner Family series. Even though I invented family history, characters, tree, and all, this was the 57th member so she had some givens to begin with. Additional story bits were made up by her anticipated owner. She had to be "on stage" during the period 1900-1910. This meant a very flamboyant version of a "My Fair Lady" costume. She had to have the "S" curve silhouette and she most definitely had to have a great big hat. I consulted my costume books and found design elements that would combine to show my concept.

■ Detail of *The Opera Singer*.

Costume always starts with the body form. You should know what era and what shape your costume will be and have a general notion when you sculpt. The body may be built to work with separate parts. In this case, I was not sure if my lady would have a high-neck or off-shoulder costume so I sculpted shoulders just in case.

With applied costume, the body can serve as a corset, and parts which do not show do not have to be made. In the Edwardian era, ladies wore corsets constructed to give them maximum bust, a wasp waist, and a large derriere. I constructed the body by assembling the paper clay parts on a wire armature. The armature was bent, then tightly wrapped "mummy" style with layers of one-inch felt strips laid so that the "S" curve appeared. A final wrapping of one-inch strips of quilt batting completed the shaping, thus eliminating the need to construct a corset. Final strength was given by a hand-sewn skin of felt.

In any costuming job, there is the point where you commune with your "stuff." To design costumes discussed here, I pulled out all the fabrics I thought would work together—basic costume, trim, lining, lace, accents such as scarves—then using a good light, sorted until I had a satisfactory combination of colors and textures. It makes a dreadful mess, but it has to be done. Decisions on fabrics, pattern balance, and texture should be mostly made before starting. Sometimes this brings serendipitous results. Making what I call an initial draping will show you what you need to find in your stash or get (such as "smooth silk needs a fine lace").

■ Susanna Oroyan, *The Opera Singer,* 18 inches, cloth.
Photo by W. Donald Smith.

1

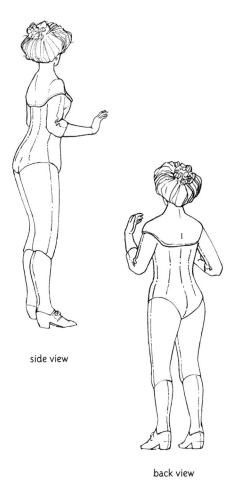

side view

back view

2

Pull the sheer fabric around leg so that it just meets at center back and then is trimmed along center back with no overlap.

Sculpt the foot in the form of a shoe last with a heel. Stockings sewn of tubes of white panty hose material went on first.

3

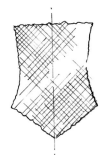

The cut stocking fabric takes the shape as shown.

4

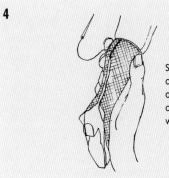

Seam the stocking at center back with tiny overcast stitches. Just catch edges of fabric with the needle.

5

As the seam is stitched, trim away any excess fabric to reduce seam bulk.

6

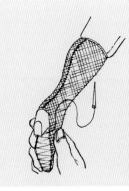

Pull the stocking fabric smoothly over the foot top and trim so that it falls to the line of the foot bottom. Then, tack in place by making zigzag stitches across bottom of the foot.

7

Form the shoe upper from a piece of soft leather.

8

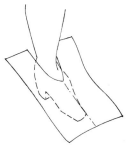

Slash and pull the shoe leather around the foot to determine the line of the heel seam. Cut the bottom line roughly to shape of foot.

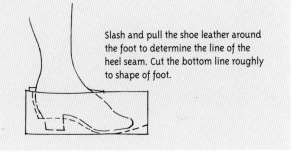

9

The basic shape of the shoe upper.

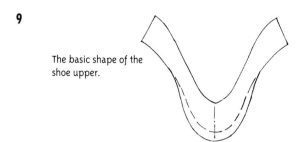

10

Machine sew the heel seam to the foot, trim exactly to the line of the heel and with a $1/8$-inch wrapping under the sole.

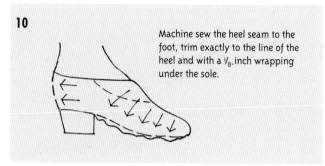

11

Stitch the edges of the upper in a zigzag manner to pull edges under foot and create a smooth surface on the foot. Any gathered material on the sole is clipped so that leather lies flat to sole.

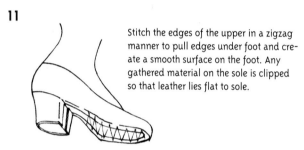

12

Wrap the heel with leather and trim so that it wraps around to the inside.

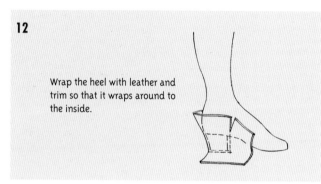

13

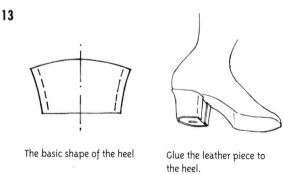

The basic shape of the heel   Glue the leather piece to the heel.

14

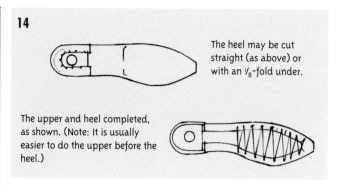

The heel may be cut straight (as above) or with an $1/8$-fold under.

The upper and heel completed, as shown. (Note: It is usually easier to do the upper before the heel.)

15

Add trims such as straps that go between sole and upper leather.

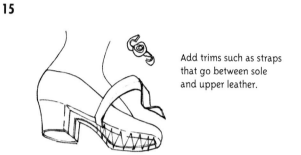

16

Make the sole for the heel by gluing a piece of leather to the bottom of the heel and trimming it flush with the edge of the heel. (Note: If the heel has been constructed with a hole for a base pin connection, the heel sole leather should be punched before gluing.)

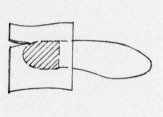

17

Alternate method:
Make a sole for the front of the foot that wraps around the heel by gluing a piece of leather to the sole and trimming it flush.

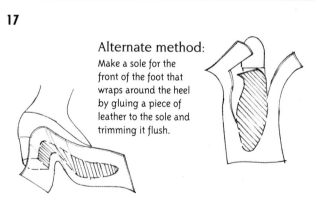

18

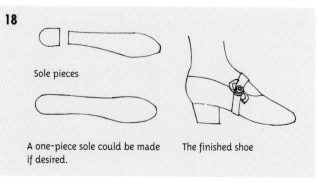

Sole pieces

A one-piece sole could be made if desired.   The finished shoe

19

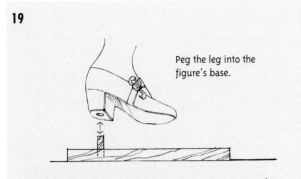

Peg the leg into the figure's base.

I drilled holes in the heels of the shoes so that the figure could be pegged in and out of a base to stand without external support. While working, I can peg the figure into a temporary wood base on a turntable.

Underwear comes next. The drawers of the era were quite fine and very daintily made. Ditto petticoats. The chemise, usually worn over the drawers and under the corset, was eliminated because the upper part would not show on the completed figure. As people are always curious to see what goes under skirts, the drawers and petticoat were made of fine batiste with lace insertion, tucks, and ribbon trim.

20

Pin fabric for the underwear to the figure along the center line of the front and back from waist to crotch. Trim so that the fabric piece allows for a $1/4$-inch seam. Note the underwear is brought above waist to the bust line to eliminate bulk at the waist.

fold line

Determine the angle of the leg by eye and cut to allow for a seam as well. Cut two pieces.

21

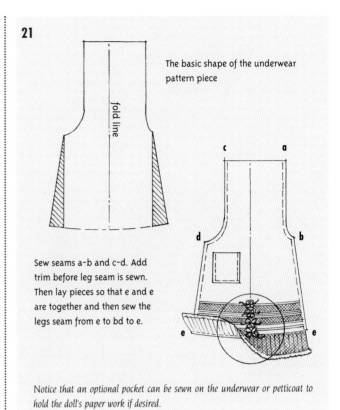

The basic shape of the underwear pattern piece

Sew seams a-b and c-d. Add trim before leg seam is sewn. Then lay pieces so that e and e are together and then sew the legs seam from e to bd to e.

Notice that an optional pocket can be sewn on the underwear or petticoat to hold the doll's paper work if desired.

22

Sew the bottom ruffle with right sides together and turn so that raw edge is to inside. Two rows of flat lace with an edge topping of $1/8$-inch grosgrain ribbon was hand sewn to the underwear. An additional line of $1/8$-inch grosgrain ribbon was added below. Tiny ribbon bows were sewn on for accent.

Trim layers for the umbrella, drawers, and petticoat were constructed as separate pieces so they could be sewn flat on the machine or by hand. Don't be afraid to sew by hand—it's surprisingly quick and more often than not, more satisfactorily exact. Petticoats, drawers, and skirts can be gathered at the top and hand sewn to the waist (as waistbands only add bulk.) With this particular costume, it was better to eliminate fullness in the top of the undergarments so that the skirt would fit smoothly over the waist and hips. Always remember that you don't have to do what cannot be seen, especially if it will adversely affect the final fit.

23

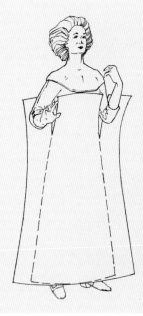

Pin the petticoat fabric to the figure to determine the petticoat front piece. Cut side seams as close to the hip and torso as possible. (Again, bring top line above waist to eliminate waist bulk.) Trim away excess fabric to make a slightly angled line from top to bottom.

Cut away excess fabric to shape petticoat front piece.

24

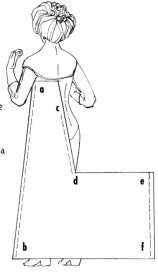

Cut the petticoat back piece with the lines at the sides, matching the front. Since the look of the era requires a train, but the dress is intended to fit smoothly to the knee, allow extra width for this at the back.

25

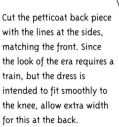

Sew the front and back pieces together at the side seams ab. The back is sewn cd and ef (de is not sewn). Turn under the seam allowance and press. Slip the petticoat on the body and tack it along the bust line. The train was pleated (or gathered) and tacked to the petticoat.

26

Finish the petticoat by closing the upper opening with overcast stitches and covering the top of the train with a bow (which will add fullness to the train). Three lines of gathered lace were added to the bottom.

■ Detail of *The Opera Singer*

27

Pin the dress fabric to the body, fitting snugly over the hips. Mark darts in front to take in excess fabric in waist area.

Cut away excess fabric to create dress front piece.

28

Pin, dart and sew the dress back pieces to the front piece. A gusseted insert was cut and sewn into the lower back seam to form the train. The opening at the back (just enough to pull dress over figure) was sewn closed with ladder stitch and the dress was tacked to the doll just under the breastplate.

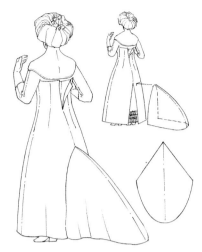

29

Determine the sleeve width and length by laying the fabric around the arm and cutting a rough rectangle with a cap. In this case, the upper arm width was the same as the hand so the sleeve could be machine sewn and pulled over the hand.

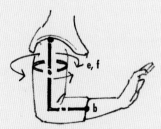

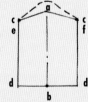

In cases where the hand shape is too large for a narrow sleeve design, the sleeve has to be hand seamed. The *Opera Singer's* dress of lavender taffeta was overlaid with lavender tulle. The tulle was pinned over the dress to the center back where it was seamed by hand. (This is done simply by holding the fabric in place while cutting.)

The sleeve cap was cut low as the edge only needs to turn under and be tacked to the figure at the top.

30

Trim the bodice by gathering and tacking a length of chiffon around the shoulders.

The droopy bustline of the Edwardian costume was "faked" by gathering and draping a chiffon panel.

Hat Assembly

31

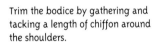

Attach the hat brim of buckram to a gathered crown of chiffon.

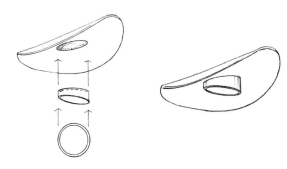

In order to make the hat tilt in a "fetching" manner, sew an angled circular support to the inside of the crown. This makes the hat tilt forward without falling over the figure's face. At this point apply the hair and cover the hat base with a base layer of chiffon. Then place the hat on the head, adjusting for the best angle. Place trims by pinning and moving ribbons and flowers until a satisfactory arrangement is decided. Then stitch all into place. The hat itself is made to be removable and is held in place with—what else—hat pins!

Finishing the costume from this point can take some time. Usually, I pin trims and accessories in place and move them around until I find a happy arrangement. For instance, the layer of puffed tulle at the bottom was pinned and re-pinned over the course of several days before it was finally tacked into place.

Costume Two: *The Nabob*

In order for my family to have enough money to be eccentric, I had to make up some stories about how they got it. This, in turn, prompted character ideas such as "the one who found Crusader treasure" and "the one who was the Elizabethan gentleman pirate." The third (and unfortunately last) infusion of funds to this fabled family came from the ancestor who made a fortune in the very early days of the British Raj in India. This character, I call *George Augustus Frederick St. John Mulliner* or *The Nabob*, who existed several years just as a name on the paper family tree.

Understanding his character (or inventing it) and his historical placement provides the initial sketch or visualization. In my story invention, *The Nabob* was an English gentleman who went to India and made a fortune in the early days of trade. He is very self-assured, very well-to-do (stinking rich and pompous) so his body stance and shape reflect his success and positive nature. (He is fat and he struts.) His tailoring reflects both his personal adaptation to local fashions and, because he has been out of the fashion loop, his suit is eccentrically out of style. He also fancies himself as a military type. This means that I can make his costume of very rich and exotic looking fabrics. I can use a turban and jewels; I can use a slightly earlier coat style with a later style of trousers. As an outdoors/military type he can also wear boots and they can be funny-looking as well. Since I especially want an exaggerated, comic effect, I don't have to follow the fashion of the era as exactly as I might if I were doing a young Benjamin Franklin. I can mix and match elements.

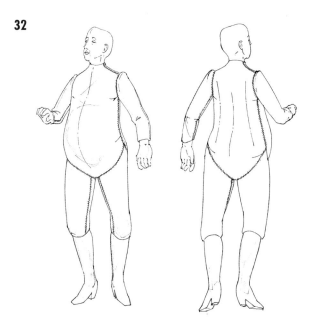

■ Susanna Oroyan, *George Augustus Frederick St. John Mulliner, Lord Poole (The Nabob)*—Mulliner Family Series, 18 inches, Super Sculpey. Photo by W. Donald Smith.

32

The Body

The head, hands, and legs are sculpted of Super Sculpey, painted and assembled on a wire armature wrapped with felt batting and covered with a hand stitched cloth skin. The figure is posed and balanced so he can stand on his own two feet without support. For security, the figure is made so that it can be pegged into a base with a rod through the shoe heels.

33

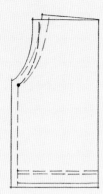

Following Rule 2, work from the inside out. Since this figure will not wear underwear, we start with his trousers. (I know that it will be nearly impossible to pull trousers over a finished boot top.) If a stocking would show, it would be the first thing to do. In the case of boots, you only need a stocking if it can be seen when someone looks down the boot. Wrap and pin fabric around the body and cut the piece with curves to accommodate back and front bulges.

Machine sew the trouser seams and put on. Decide the length of leg, trim and gather. Turn the gathers under, adjust and sew the trouser leg directly to the knee. Tuck excess fabric at the waist to form a pleat. To reduce bulk, there is no turn under of raw edges at the waist. No part of the waist of the pants will show when the costume is finished. Rule 3: don't do it if you don't have to.

Boots

34

Construct the heel and upper part of boot in the same manner as the *Opera Singer's* shoes. Notice that the foot itself is sculpted to form a square-toed shoe last. To reflect military boots of that era, I added a trim of contrasting leather around the sole line.

35

All the boot leather came from only one old glove. The boot tops were formed from glove fingers which added a seamed texture. As the fingers were not quite wide enough to go around the calf, I had to "fudge" by inserting a tongue at the back, held in place by knotted leather. To make the design more interesting, I pinked small strips of the leather to trim the boot top. In the fashion of the day, a stirrup strap and chain were added at the ankle and a decorative leather bow at the front. All trims used the reverse side of the leather so two textures and color shades were gained from the same leather.

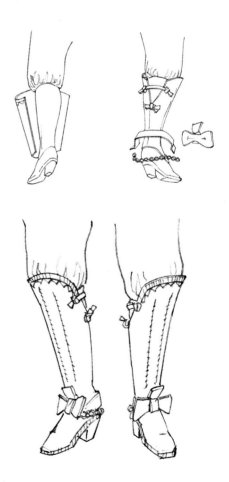

■ Detail of *The Nabob*

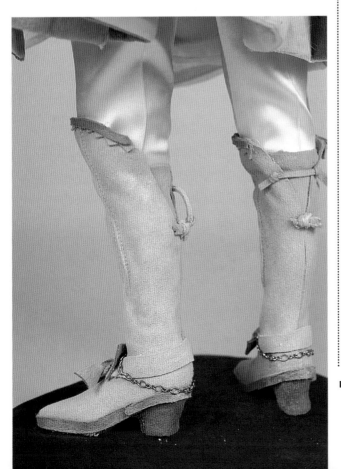

Shirt

36

Our 18th century gent would have worn a big, long, full-sleeved shirt made of linen. Even if we scaled this correctly by using a lightweight batiste, it would still create unnecessary bulk under the coat so I built a fake cuff and added a neckcloth later.

37

Vest

Since the figure will wear a long, full-skirted coat, he will not need the back half of his vest. It will be just an appliquéd fake front. With reference to the source material for length and shape, I pinned fabric to the body along center line of front and at the side, and cut the vest-front shape by eye. I cut so that a 1/4-inch seam is allowed.

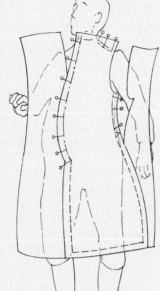

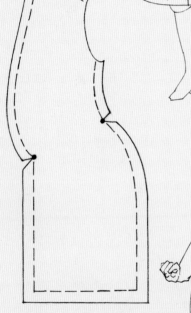

The basic shape of the vest

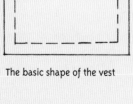

38

The vest will need lining as the inside will show.

39

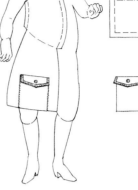

Cut, sew, trim and attach a pocket to the vest with hidden stitches.

40

Lap the two vest fronts at the center and stitch to the body. Note: to reduce bulk, only the finished side (top) is turned under along the seam allowance. The underside is left flat.

41

Tack the vest to the side of the figure.

42

Hand sew trims to complete the vest.

43

Pin coat fabric to the back of the figure along the center back, side, and top to fit as smoothly as possible across the widest areas at shoulder and hip. Take in loose fabric in the waist area by placing a dart. Since the style chosen has boxed pleats at the center back and sides, cut the pattern to allow for a deep pleat.

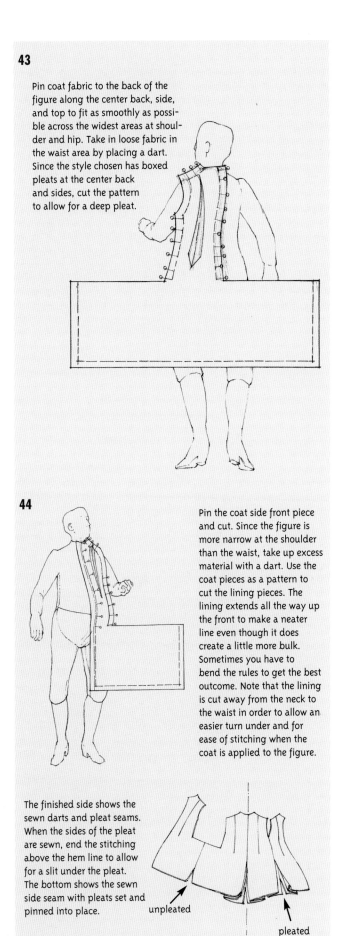

44

Pin the coat side front piece and cut. Since the figure is more narrow at the shoulder than the waist, take up excess material with a dart. Use the coat pieces as a pattern to cut the lining pieces. The lining extends all the way up the front to make a neater line even though it does create a little more bulk. Sometimes you have to bend the rules to get the best outcome. Note that the lining is cut away from the neck to the waist in order to allow an easier turn under and for ease of stitching when the coat is applied to the figure.

The finished side shows the sewn darts and pleat seams. When the sides of the pleat are sewn, end the stitching above the hem line to allow for a slit under the pleat. The bottom shows the sewn side seam with pleats set and pinned into place.

unpleated

pleated

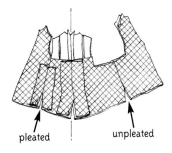

pleated   unpleated

When the work shown (left) is turned over, you can see the set, stitched, and pressed pleats. Stitch the pleat-folds to the lining across the top and about an inch down each side to hold them in place.

45

Add pockets and put the assembled coat on the figure. Adjust to achieve desired hang of the skirt and fall of the front coat opening. Turn under the front along the front edge and sew the shoulder seam.

Adjust front view of the coat for hang and line. Once the "look" has been determined by pinning the coat in place, sew it to the body. To make the coat stay permanently in place, stitch it to the body along the side seam from underneath. Tack each front in place as well. Additionally, the skirts may be flipped up and the coat tacked to the body across the back at the waistline. The idea is that subsequent handling cannot disturb the drape of the coat, and if the coat tails are lifted, all parts visible are neat with no raw edges or unfinished body parts showing.

46

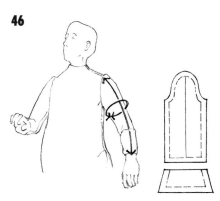

Measure the arm and cut a sleeve and cuff. If the sleeve seam is to be machine sewn, be sure to cut the sleeve wide enough to be able to pull the stitched piece over the hand. When the fingers are in a spread out position, you are either forced to make a wide sleeve or to hand sew the seam with the fabric on the figure.

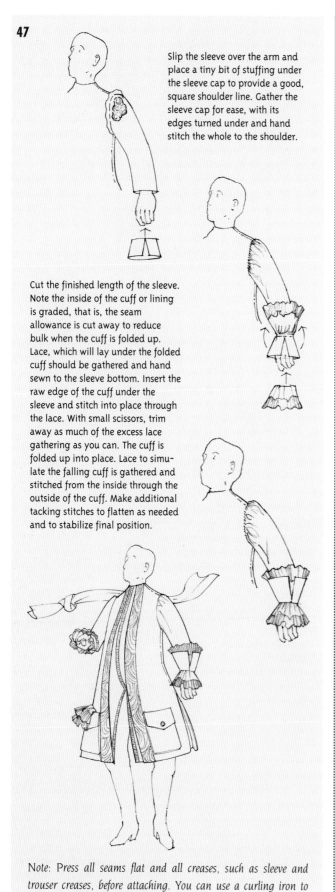

47

Slip the sleeve over the arm and place a tiny bit of stuffing under the sleeve cap to provide a good, square shoulder line. Gather the sleeve cap for ease, with its edges turned under and hand stitch the whole to the shoulder.

Cut the finished length of the sleeve. Note the inside of the cuff or lining is graded, that is, the seam allowance is cut away to reduce bulk when the cuff is folded up. Lace, which will lay under the folded cuff should be gathered and hand sewn to the sleeve bottom. Insert the raw edge of the cuff under the sleeve and stitch into place through the lace. With small scissors, trim away as much of the excess lace gathering as you can. The cuff is folded up into place. Lace to simulate the falling cuff is gathered and stitched from the inside through the outside of the cuff. Make additional tacking stitches to flatten as needed and to stabilize final position.

Note: Press all seams flat and all creases, such as sleeve and trouser creases, before attaching. You can use a curling iron to press some parts after assembly.

The Little Last Things

Once the basic ensemble is completed, the fun begins. Between coat assembly and sleeves, I had to make some final decisions about trims. Although I had a fair idea of what I was going to do, I spent several days laying out possible combinations of braids, lace, buttons, sash materials, and jewelry. I pin the materials to the figure and move them around so that final placement and drape for the entire costume can be worked together. *The Nabob*, as a comic character, actually requires the addition of funny but authentic extras.

We reckon *The Nabob's* period to be roughly 1725. At that time, men rarely wore their hair loose, but remember *The Nabob* is behind the times. He gets the long hairstyle of a few years earlier and it has a ribbon-tied lovelock. To top him off in keeping with the Eastern potentate image, he wears a turban of combined colored silks. An earring, well, naturally!

The neckcloth was a rather important piece of dress. Our character would have worn his neckcloth tied in several ways and even lopped through his lapel.

In *The Nabob's* era, handkerchiefs were used as decorative dress and for emphasis in conversation. I gave him a nice, big lacy one.

If one is good, two might be better, so *The Nabob* gets two colorful sashes and a big braided sword knot. A walking stick was also an important part of gent's dress at this time.

Of course, he had a decorative order and a medal is pinned to his chest. He probably thought he deserved one or two more so we hang some around his neck.

Important to the story of *The Nabob's* wealth is the fabulous ruby and pearl pendent. The pearl came from the Crusader's treasure and the ruby, of course, from his India trade.

Most of the Mulliner family of figures bring a little fun to their owners. They collect things. In his new home, *The Nabob's* owner is busily adding chests of jewels and coins to his trivia. *The Opera Singer* we have on good authority—will be a multi-faceted collector (Mulliners want it all). She is probably going to want teddy bears, tea sets, and examples of fine needlework.

To review the four basic rules:

- Reduce bulk.

- Work from the inside out.

- Don't do it if you don't have to.

- Finish all parts that will be seen.

■ Susanna Oroyan, *Bunny Forbes*,
18 inches, Super Sculpey.
Photo by W. Donald Smith.

■ Susanna Oroyan, *Mrs. Hudson Holmes*,
18 inches, Super Sculpey.
Photo by W. Donald Smith.

■ Susanna Oroyan, *Morelock Mulliner* and *Dotson Forbes*,
18 inches, Super Sculpey.
Photo by W. Donald Smith.

■ Susanna Oroyan, *Phil Forbes*,
18 inches, Super Sculpey.
Photo by W. Donald Smith.

■ Susanna Oroyan, *Daphne Mulliner,*
12 inches, Super Sculpey.
Photo by W. Donald Smith.

■ Susanna Oroyan, *Trixie Mulliner,*
18 inches, Super Sculpey.
Photo by W. Donald Smith.

■ Susanna Oroyan, *Rose Petunia,*
18 inches, Super Sculpey.
Photo by W. Donald Smith.

■ Susanna Oroyan, *Letitia Mulliner,*
18 inches, Super Sculpey.
Photo by W. Donald Smith.

■ Dan Fletcher, *Orin,* 19 inches, washi paper and La Doll.
Photo by Dan Fletcher.

■ Charles Batte, *Manon Lescaut,*
22 inches, polymer clay with cloth body.
Photo by Peter Marcus.

■ Charles Batte, *The Grand Duchess Xenia Alexandrovna,*
16 inches, polymer clay.
Photo by Peter Marcus.

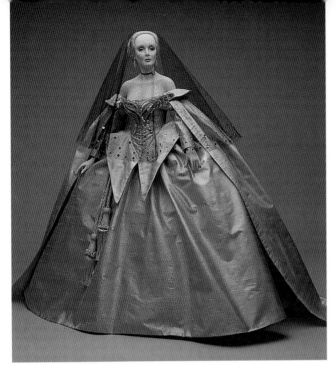

■ Paul Crees and Peter Coe, *The Golden Infanta,*
28 inches, poured wax.
Photo by Crees and Coe.

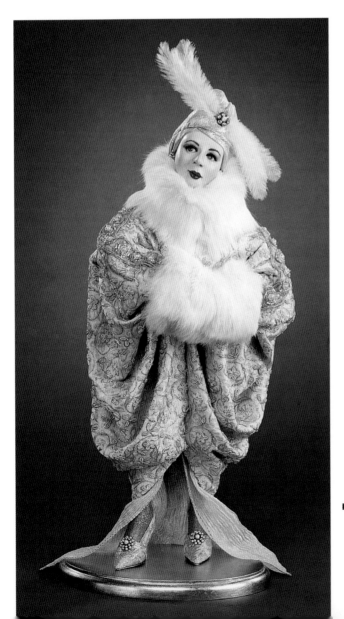

■ Paul Crees and Peter Coe, *Lestat,*
28 inches, poured wax.
Photo by Crees and Coe.

■ Charles Batte, *Pauline St. Clair,* 18 inches, polymer clay.
Photo by Peter Marcus.

■ Paul Crees and Peter Coe, *Ghost of Versailles,*
28 inches, poured wax.
Photo by Crees and Coe.

■ Antonette Cely, *Here Comes the Bride,* 16 inches, cloth.
Photo by Don Cely.

■ Paul Crees and Peter Coe, *The Buttercup Bride,*
28 inches, poured wax.
Photo by Crees and Coe.

■ Sandra Wright Justiss, *Julia,* 16 inches, paper clay.
Photo by Jerry Anthony.

■ Sandra Wright Justiss, *African Baroque,* 16 inches, paper clay.
Photo by Jerry Anthony.

■ Sandra Wright Justiss, *Medusa,* 16 inches, paper clay.
Photo by Jerry Anthony.

■ Akiko Anzai, *Judith,* 14 inches, cloth.
Photo by Akiko Anzai.

■ Antonette Cely, *Midnight Rendezvous,* 18 inches, cloth.
Photo by Don Cely.

■ Dorothy Hoskins, *Another Story,*
7 inches, direct sculpture, porcelain.
Photo by Pauline Chamness.

■ Dan Fletcher, *Nagaya no Asa,* 13 inches, washi paper and La Doll.
Photo by Dan Fletcher.

■ Patti Bibb, *Queen Ant's Lace,* 18 inches, paper clay over cloth. Photo by W. Donald Smith.

■ Gail Lackey, *Madame and the Marquis,* 18 inches, Super Sculpey. Photo by Matt McKain.

■ Dimitri Zurilkin, *Time to Eat Rice,* 23 cm, La Doll, silk. Photo by Victor Chernishov.

■ Kathryn Walmsley, *The Deer Maiden,* 17 inches, Cernit. Photo by Kathryn Walmsley.

■ Detail of *Queen Elizabeth I*

■ George Stuart, *Queen Elizabeth I,* 18 inches, mixed media.
Photo by Peter D'Aprix.

■ Marina Guseva, *Seasons: Autumn*,
70 cm, clay, textile.
Photo by Viktor Chernishov.

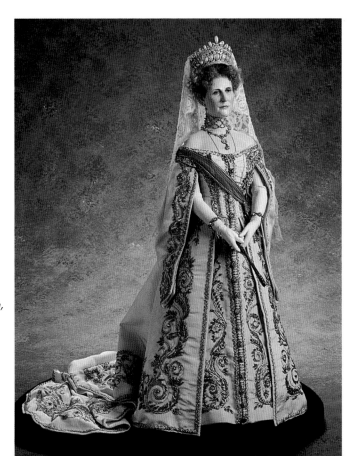

■ George Stuart, *Empress Alexandra of Russia,*
18 inches, mixed media.
Photo by Peter D'Aprix.

■ Chris Chomick and Peter Meder, *Balthazar the Judicator,*
21 inches, Cernit, wood armature.
Photo by Chris Chomick.

■ Nancy J. Laverick, *Basil the Bass Player,*
14 inches, cloth.
Photo by James Christensen.

■ Lisa L. Lichtenfels, *The Last Samaritan,*
29 inches, nylon needlesculpture.
Photo by Lisa L. Lichtenfels.

■ Sherry Housley, *Renegade,*
14 inches, Super Sculpey.
Photo by Sherry Housley.

■ Anya Lewis, *Tsyganochki—Russian Gyspy Children,*
12 inches, Cernit.
Photo by Phillip Jones.

■ Bronwyn Hayes, *Amelia,* 36 cm, cloth over wire armature.
Photo by David Reid.

■ Gillie Charlson, *Biddy and Becky,* 23 inches, porcelain.
Photo by Gillie Charlson.

■ Svetlana Voskressenskaya, *Margarita,* 70 cm, porcelain. Photo by Victor Chernishov.

■ Mary Jo Carpenter, *Spring,* 14 inches, Super Sculpey. Photo by Mary Jo Carpenter.

■ Elena Nassedkina, *Inflation,* 42 cm, La Doll.
Photo by Victor Chernishov.

■ Dru Esslinger, *Where Is That Bus!,*
19 inches, fabric over armature.
Photo by Beverly Dodge Radefeld.

■ Linda Ewing, *My Little Man,* 14 inches,
paper clay, paper costume.
Photo by W. Donald Smith.

■ Mary Worrow, *Kabuki Silk Moth,* 18 inches, paper clay.
Photo by Mary Worrow.

■ Dorothy Hoskins, *April,* 6 inches, porcelain, direct sculpture.
Photo by Pauline Chamness.

■ Dorothy Hoskins, *Balancing Act,* 8 inches, porcelain.
Photo by Pauline Chamness.

■ Paul Crees and Peter Coe, *Fox Lady,* 27 inches, poured wax.
Photo by Crees and Coe.

■ Alessandra White, *Rose,* 24 inches, cloth.
Photo by Jerry Anthony.

■ Gillie Charlson, *Elizabeth Bowes Lyon,* 16 inches, porcelain.
Photo by Gillie Charlson.

■ Carla Thompson, *Winter Dream,* 18 inches,
cloth with cloth head.
Photo by Carla Thompson.

■ Donna May Robinson, *Sister's Sunday Best,*
16 inches, oil-painted cloth.
Photo by Jerry Anthony.

■ Debbie Richmond, *Nellie,* 20 inches, leather and felt. Photo by Denny Richmond.

■ Ethel Loh Strickarz, *Painting the Who,* 20 inches, La Doll. Photo by William G. Moogan.

■ Susan Fosnot, *Maidi,* 21 inches, oil-painted cloth. Photo by Ann Nevills.

■ Susan Fosnot, *Baby,* 18 inches, oil-painted cloth. Photo by Ann Nevills.

■ Joyce Patterson, *Carmen Miranda,*
17 inches, cloth.
Photo by Joyce Patterson.

■ Willemijn van der Spiegel, *Dutchgirls,* 45 cm,
impregnated fabric, wood paste.
Photo by Ad van den Brink.

■ Pattie Bibb, *Hatterpillar,* 18 inches,
paper clay over cloth.
Photo by W. Donald Smith.

■ Julie McCullough, *Hilda,* 15 inches, cloth.
Photo by John Nollendorf.

■ Stephanie Blythe, *Amorous Liaisons,* 10 inches, porcelain.
Photo by Hap Sakwa.

■ Stephanie Blythe, *Lovers-Undressed,* 10 inches,
molded and direct-sculpted porcelain.
Photo by Hap Sakwa.

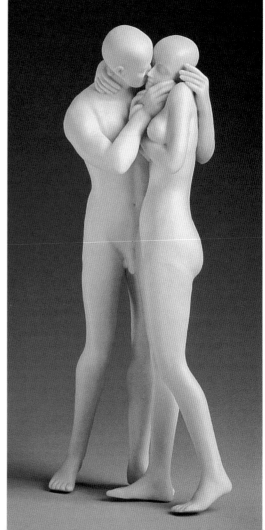

CHAPTER FOUR

The Elements
of Costume

How do I compress several thousand years of fashion in hundreds of ethnic styles into one chapter? The answer is, I can't. Much as I would like to take a trip through all the wonderful shapes, styles, and exciting details, it just isn't possible in this format. Fortunately, others have done encyclopedic works on the subject and you can find them in your bookshop and library. I can, however, provide an overview of the importance of shape and line with a few hints as to how a doll maker can achieve a good, believable look in costume.

In case you are tempted to skip this part because you do characters or abstracts, think again. Some of these things are as important to you as to the historical costumer. Some of the effects of fantasy and "far out" costume are simply old tricks re-shaped.

When I costumed the *Opera Singer*, my initial goal was to portray the shape of Edwardian style, the "S" curve. When I costumed *The Nabob*, my objective was to make the clothing emphasize the comic character. In both cases—realistic and character—shape and form were crucial to getting the idea across. The same is true when I work on an impressionistic or abstract figure. If I set out to do a tubular figure with little or no muscular definition and a bland face, the lines of the costume will be broadly straight, square, or circular. I would not consider doing a detailed ruffled skirt and fussy lace, puff-sleeved costume on that shape. If I set out to do a fantasy character, I will build the costume to reflect the person in his or her world. Almost none of the costumes for the empresses shown in the beginning of this book relate to reality. No real person could function wearing them, however, if you are an Intergalactic Empress (whatever that might be) you probably don't have to walk, sit, or push a vacuum cleaner. Even so, the empresses' costumes convey their personae. If you didn't know the names of the dolls, you would probably still think, airy, hot, earthy, just by the color and the form. I hope.

Sometimes costuming is just plain mind games. The *Atmospheric Empress* (page 103) may not immediately identify herself without a title and, yet, her costume reflects rain, snow, ice, hail and clouds. I have also done the ultimate non-doll. That is a doll costumed, so to speak, in a black bag. You have to feel it to know it's a doll.

■ Willemijn van der Spiegel, *Adum* detail, 45 cm, impregnated fabric.
Photo by Ad van den Brink.

All in all, the goal is a believable piece. The viewer should get somewhere near accepting the idea you had in mind.

How you do that is by learning a great deal about the elements of historical costume and, because fabrics and materials don't always scale down, by using an equal amount of construction trickery, deceit, and deviousness. In short, no matter what type of a figure you are making, you have to learn to fake the reality to make it a reality.

The easiest way to see this is in a realistic or historical figure. You spend much time sculpting clay or designing and cutting fabric to create a body that conforms to human proportions— that looks like a real naked person. Then, you try to put it into Elizabethan costume and it just doesn't look right. Why? Because Elizabethan (and 18th century and Victorian, etc.) costume did not conform to a real human body. In every era, with the possible exception of ours, clothing has reflected style preferences, concepts of class and the needs of climate. Those preferences have accentuated or minimized certain body parts and required specific materials. As a result, for the doll costumer, there are two important guidelines. The higher the class, the more difficult the clothing will be to move in. The idea is that if you are rich, others move around for you. The higher the class, the richer the materials and the heavier the embellishment. The idea here is that if you have it, you show it off. A man today would do about anything to hide a potbelly and accentuate his shoulders. A man of the Renaissance padded his doublet to show he could afford warmth, to show he was well enough off to eat sumptuously, and if he were rich, he didn't have to have shoulder muscles for working.

To get the right look for a costume means that you have to make the body the shape you want the costume. Or you have to add to the body or the costume to change the final outline. It also means that if you want historical authenticity, you become something of a scholar. No matter how much you like ruffled petticoats and underwear, a colonial lady living in a cold house would most likely have worn a chemise (no underpants) with knit petticoat and a quilted petticoat and maybe more than two petticoats. When you make a costume with this kind of thoroughness, the viewer is more surprised and delighted with your unique piece.

Some things to remember:

- Knitting is known from the second century CE and was probably done before that in Egypt.

- Lace is known to have been made in ancient times, but was refined in the late Middle Ages in mediterranean countries.

- Hook and eye fastenings have been used since Medieval times.

- Eyeglasses appear to have come into use about 1200-1300.

- Button/buttonhole closures came into use in the 1400s.

- Shoes for men and women were pretty much the same in shape and style until the 1600s.

- Knitting machines for stockings were invented and put into use between 1600-1700.

- Shoes were not made for left and right feet until the 1800s.

- The zipper was first manufactured in the 1920s.

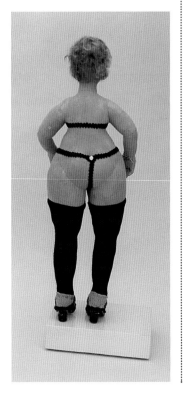

Most of this happens beneath the final layer so let's start with underwear.

Underwear

Shimmy, skinny, sark to shirt

If a doll with a skirted costume is not fixed to a base, the viewer will look underneath. This is a rule. People are just curious. Remember the rule: If any part of the piece can been seen, it must be given a complete and neat finish. There is a corollary here, too. Most people see dolls or figures as people, and they like pieces that have legs even if they are not exposed. This means nice underwear if the outer clothing can be moved to expose limbs underneath. Of course, underwear has not always been worn. If it is not appropriate to the historical era or the cultural milieu of your character, you don't have to do it. If it is, then make it just as interesting as the outer, immediately visible layer.

But how do we know what kind of underwear? We don't. Since it was not a subject of literature, illustration, or general conversation until modern times, we can only guess from those artworks of an era which might show semi-naked subjects. For most of Europe and the Mediterranean, from pre-history to at least 1000 CE it seems the basic rule was none or shirttails. What appears to be bra and shorts in Roman paintings of athletes, is probably more like a bandeau and loincloth which might have been costume as much as clothing. Additional clothing for warmth was usually layered on top rather than underneath. And, let's face it, for the majority, toilet facilities were such that unwrapping cloth or dealing with drawers under long skirts wouldn't have been very efficient.

From early times, in most cultures, men seem to have worn a piece of cloth wrapped sarong-style around the waist, pulled up between their legs and tucked into the waist.

Later, their hose extended to the waist with front and back closed with lacings. The idea of a trouser cut or seamed crotch with legs seems to have come from the East through riding cultures and could have been used from the time of the Eastern invasions in the Roman Era.

As the trouser cut developed, underwear, referred to as small clothes, were just that—simple versions made in lighter weight fabrics than outer trousers. Long underwear and boxer style shorts for men at first developed with the sewing machine; jockey shorts, singlets, and tee shirts came later with the tricot knitting machine.

■ Beverly Dodge Radefeld, *Thank You, Victoria*, 22 inches, cloth.
Photo by Beverly Dodge Radefeld.

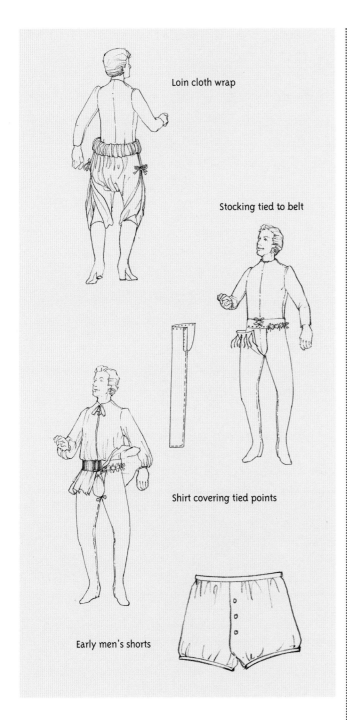

Loin cloth wrap

Stocking tied to belt

Shirt covering tied points

Early men's shorts

that time we also see some developments in fireplaces and chimneys. At the same time, clothing for both sexes became multi-layered.

The Scotsman's plaid or what we think of as the kilt is a good example of draped clothing without underwear. In earlier days, a length of woolen was woven as wide as the loom—as much as 2 yards wide and 6 yards long. When the Scot dressed, he put on his shirt (if he had one), which was a lighter woven wool or linen extending to mid-thigh. Then, he laid his wide leather belt on the ground and pleated the woolen length over it. He laid down on the fabric, picked up one end of the belt and rolled himself up into the fabric and buckled the belt. The leftover length above the belt on the right was pulled up and pinned at the shoulder. The other part of the top was tucked into the belt or pulled over the head to form a sort of cape and hood for all-weather protection. The mid-calf length allowed the wearer, male or female, to work outdoors with easier movement and without the bother of muddy bottom edges. Similar belted lengths of cloth, from sari to sarong, were worn, and still are, by many people around the world.

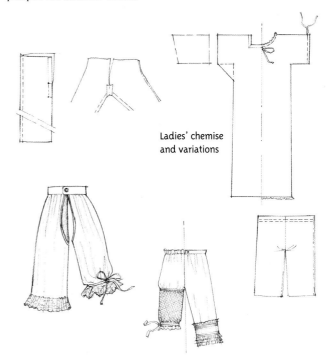

Ladies' chemise and variations

Ladies' slit drawers: each leg shows a different finish style.

Women who wore long and voluminous skirts do not seem to have commonly worn anything like modern underwear until the thinner fabrics and slim lines in clothing of the early 1800s dictated a need to cover up with a pair of under-drawers or pantalets. Even then many were made split to accommodate commodes. Until that period typical women's undergarments were versions of the chemise—essentially long tunics—and petticoats. Weather is another factor. It seems that from Biblical times to about 1000 CE the climate of Western Europe was somewhat warmer. (Perhaps one of the reasons Europeans lost the Roman art of central heating.) Approximately 1100 CE, things began to cool a bit, and at

To review, there are two considerations for underwear. First, if it is used for historical costume then it should be appropriate to the era. For instance, a medieval princess would not wear pantalets. Second, if it is used on a non-dressable doll, only the part that shows needs to be made. This means that if the bodice of a costume is to be sewn to the body, you don't have to construct a full chemise, bra, or slip top. For male figures wearing attached trousers, if the body has not been sculpted or constructed to show sexed detail, artists often pad the crotch area to achieve a correct-looking drape for trousers.

Many people think that a figure just ought to be covered below the waist for purposes of modesty. If that is the case, you can suggest underwear in a sculpted figure by making the sculpture non-detailed or sculpting lines to suggest cloth and coloring the material. On a fabric figure, you can vary the body fabric. (For example, use white fabric above the knee or mid-thigh.)

Underpinnings

All Shaped Up

After the chemise or shirt comes foundation wear. These are the shapers and extenders that create the outline of a particular fashion. These are the hoops and cages that went on over the chemise and before the petticoat or the pads that were built into tops and sleeves. It is important to note that almost all of these things, as well as over-clothing like trousers and dresses, were pretty much what we would call separates. The notion of a closet with hangers is only something that has developed in the last 100 years. Prior to that, most clothing was stored in chests or drawers or was hung on pegs. Clothing was generally constructed to be flat. The separate pieces were tied together—skirts to bodices, trousers to doublets, and then often gathered to create drapes. If you are wondering why the early tailors and dressmakers did not just sew the parts together, consider the weight and thickness of a padded velvet or brocade piece. Lacings would be far more secure in the long run.

Realistic figures will often need shoulder pads to make a costume hang correctly. Padding was often used to accentuate specific body areas. When knee britches were worn, men with thin calves, wore padded stockings.

Padding up the natural shoulder line can create the broad-shouldered form as well as direct the fall of sleeve fabric.

For the doll maker, padding under lady's clothing can be fun and simple to make. Typically, early forms of under-padding were made of cotton or linen and stuffed with cork. You can achieve the modern equivalent by crushing Styrofoam into rough pellet shapes. Some pads were stuffed with down. Not everyone wore hoops and panniers all the time.

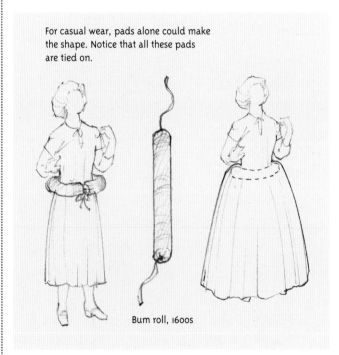

For casual wear, pads alone could make the shape. Notice that all these pads are tied on.

Bum roll, 1600s

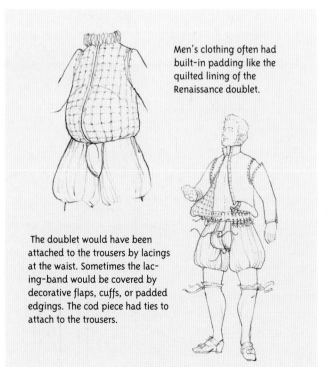

Men's clothing often had built-in padding like the quilted lining of the Renaissance doublet.

The doublet would have been attached to the trousers by lacings at the waist. Sometimes the lacing-band would be covered by decorative flaps, cuffs, or padded edgings. The cod piece had ties to attach to the trousers.

Bustle, 1780

Back pad, 1810 - attached to the dress with ties.

Bustle, 1870

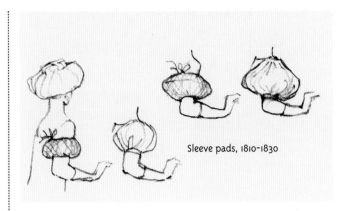

Sleeve pads, 1810-1830

Extenders

When rich brocades, satins and velvets began to become accessible in Europe about 1500, women naturally wanted to show them off. The more yardage you could show, the better. For most of us today, a full skirt means a gathered rectangular length of fabric or one cut on a circle. While circular cuts come and go in styles, gathers rarely appear until recently. Most fullness was achieved by pleats—either flat or cartridge type. Gathering heavy material limits the fullness to what can be brought into the waist—usually the waist measurement times three or a maximum of three yards. Pleating gives you lots more!

Cage Extenders

Pleating brought about the development of the farthingale, the first hooped or "cage" skirt shaper. In the next three centuries, four basic forms of the cage extender evolved. If you want your skirted figure to have any of these four shapes, even if not a historical piece, do try constructing the cage it needs to hold the shape.

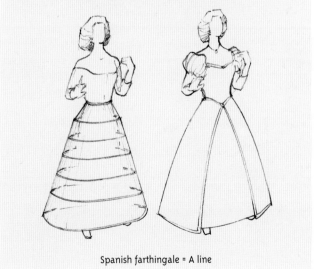

Spanish farthingale = A line

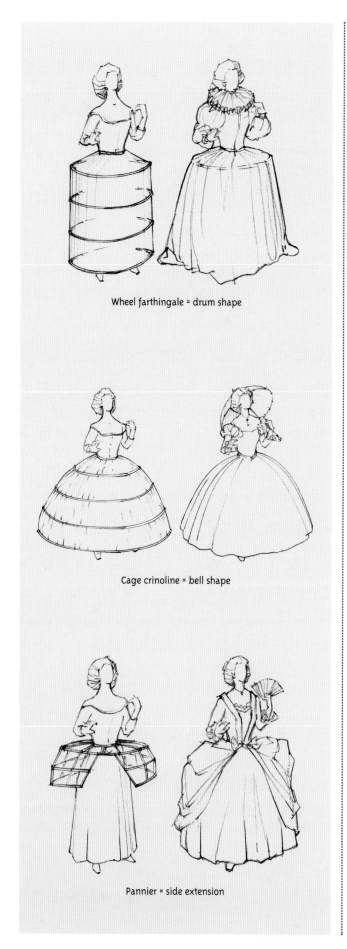

Wheel farthingale = drum shape

Cage crinoline = bell shape

Pannier = side extension

Construction Principle:

Fortunately for doll makers who like authenticity, cage extenders were as often as not made by inserting metal or reed staves into casings sewn into a cloth form. This created a lightweight wearable and, if the staves were removed, a flat-fold garment. It is also far easier for you to construct a flat piece with casings than it is to try to evenly connect wire hoops with tape.

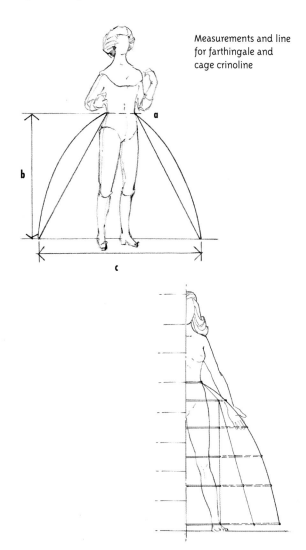

Measurements and line for farthingale and cage crinoline

1. Lay your figure flat on a piece of paper and draw the outline of the skirt shape you want.

2. For Wheel farthingale, start horizontal line at top of pelvis (a). Horizontal measurements multiplied by four will be the lengths of casing inserts.
For 1860 cage, start horizontal line between upper hip and waist.

3. Measure from waist to foot bottom to get the width (b).

4. Bottom measurement-line doubled is the length of the fabric (c).

Wheel farthingale only requires two horizontal staves/casings—one at hip and one at bottom. Spanish farthingale and cage crinoline should have four horizontal staves/casings.

Stave Material

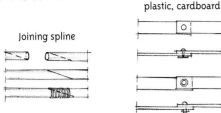

Joining spline

Joining metal, plastic, cardboard

Use round or thin flat basket spline (reed) which might be available at your craft supplier. Soak to dampen, bend if necessary. Or, cut thin strips of cardboard or plastic. Joined wire (see hat section page 79) can also be used in casings. Spring steel is also possible if you want to use nuts and bolts or solder. Note when making choice that wire and cardboard can be bent out-of-shape and spring steel is often sharp enough on edges to cut fabric.

Joins

1. Cut fabric rectangle per measurements. Use bias tape to machine-sew casings. Or, use two layers of fabric and sew parallel lines to form casings.

2. Stop casing stitching at seam line. Sew seam.

3. After casings are constructed and seams sewn, insert stave material in casing. Plastic or cardboard strips can be joined by punching a hole and fastening ends together with a brad. Lightweight cardboard and plastic can be joined by using a grommet or eyelet punch.

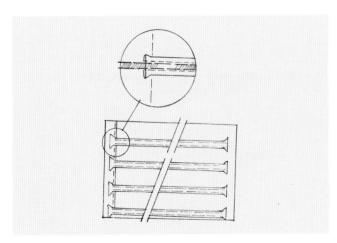

4. Insert stave material and connect ends. Hand-stitch casing ends together at seam line to close.

5. Eliminate gathered bulk at waist for cage crinoline: Hem top edge at top casing before inserting stave. Sew tapes to top row and attach by stitching to waist of figure or a cloth waist band.

Panniers

These are the side extensions that were developed from the baskets carried by donkeys. The early forms were made of basket materials. Later forms, like the hoops, were made of cloth with encased staves. Even if you are not planning a historically accurate costume, panniers are a great way to add embellishment to your figure. If you have a feeling for the "far-out," you can put baskets of flowers, fruits, toys or whatever follows your theme on these side extensions.

The pannier shape. A simple form to directly attach to a soft doll body can be made as follows:

Cut form of cardboard and cover it with fabric. Bend around doll, pin to hold, and use heavy-duty needle and thread to stitch ends together. Add tape. Stitch form to figure. Stitch through doll, if possible.

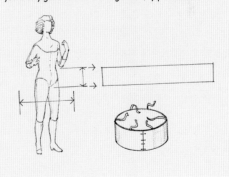

Note: A variation of the wheel farthingale can be made by cutting a rectangle of cardboard and covering it with fabric. Sew tapes to sides of front and back and at ends as shown and connect them to waist.

Folding panniers can be made by constructing a waist band of heavy cotton.

Petticoats

Enhancers

Once the form of the skirt has been set with pads or extenders, the costume then requires petticoats to reflect and enhance that shape. Now, we have to consider the cut of the cloth so that when the petticoat is constructed it does what we need it to do.

The drape of fabric over panniers will naturally lift a rectangular piece of gathered fabric. A petticoat to fit over the panniers and fall evenly will need to compensate by cutting a yoke, cutting fabric longer where it will fall over the ends, or pleating up ends.

1

Cut cardboard or plastic strips in graduated lengths. Punch hole in end of each hoop strip and in band.

2

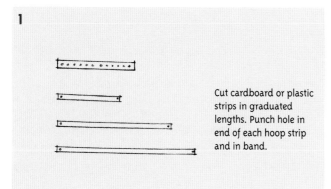

Attach strips to waist band with brad, as shown.

3

Sew tape at each side to hold in position (a, b, c)

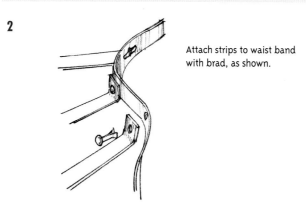

4

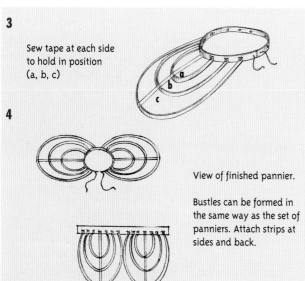

View of finished pannier.

Bustles can be formed in the same way as the set of panniers. Attach strips at sides and back.

To fit nicely over a bustle, a petticoat requires a straight front panel and a wider, perhaps ruffled back panel. Additional ruffles might be added for a trained skirt.

A circular cut petticoat will fit over a cage crinoline without adding gathered bulk at the waist.

A petticoat for a dress with a train.

The Evolution of the Dress

Putting Together the Pieces

What we would call a dress was, in earlier times, an evolved chemise—a simple, long, straight-sleeved garment. In its underwear form the chemise shape changed little.

Evolution of the dress

In its outerwear form, a chemise became an upper bodice and a lower skirt or petticoat.

As a one-piece garment it became known as a kirtle.

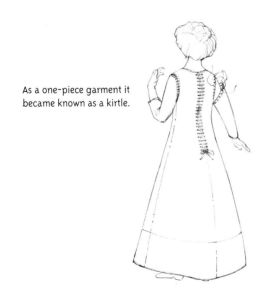

Kirtle

The kirtle was often sleeveless, laced up the back to give it a slight shaping, and worn with a coat-like loose gown over it. Sleeves were laced into the shoulders of the kirtle and longer, fuller sleeves could be laced into the loose gown. The effect is rather like what we would call a dress and coat ensemble. So by the 1500s we have the origins of the one-piece dress in the kirtle, the coat in the loose gown, and skirts and blouses in the cut apart chemise and the bodice/corset.

The modern one-piece dress also evolved from the laced attachment of skirt to bodice. This happened between 1600 and 1700. However, two-piece laced costumes were worn well into the 19th century.

Corsets

Relax, you probably won't need to make a corset, unless your design calls for one to be seen. Your figure's body sculpture and posture can take care of the shape you want to show.

The corset—sometimes called a "body" from the root word "corp"—is confusing from the start. Originally, and for much of their history, the idea has been to change the outline shape of the top of the figure by compressing the body. Corsets were usually made of heavy linen or canvas fabric. Stays or boning of reed, metal, or whalebone, were stitched trapunto style between the layers of cloth to stiffen. The placement of the stiffened "bone" material directed the final shape. And there was a specific shape for every style. Corsets either compressed the breast or left them semi-free until the mid-nineteenth century when bust accommodations were built in. Corsets are also worn on top of other underpinnings...it's the last thing before the dress and sometimes it is the upper outer garment.

The doll maker usually will not have to make a corset. What he will have to do is make the costume look as if it had one. The best way to do this is to design the doll body in the shape you want to show.

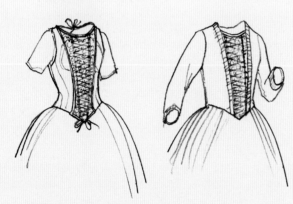

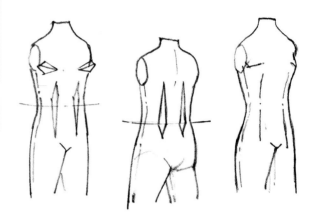

Corsets could be laced tightly together at the front or laced over a flat triangular piece of stiffened fabric called a stomacher. To further confuse us, the stomacher could be laced or hooked to an outer bodice. Fashion has always been variable and interesting in its combinations

This now one-piece garment opened at the front and was pinned or laced over the heavy-duty form-shaping corset and stomacher in the 1700s. (Note that underpinning really was pinned. Straight pins were often used to join bodice sides to stomacher.)

When you begin with the shape you want, all you need to do is cut the pieces for the top of the garment to the shape of the body. You will, however, probably want to line a bodice and add a stomacher if hard lines are desired.

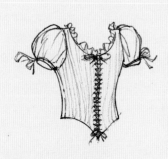

Corsets or bodies were often worn by working women as outerwear over the chemise. Much of European folk costume consists of a corset laced over a chemise with a skirt and petticoats. When the outer garment lost some of its boning and took on sleeves, the term bodice appeared. At the same time this bodice begins to become permanently attached to the skirts.

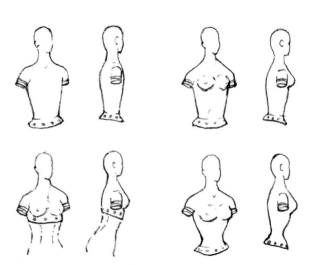

Sculpted body

Bodice Cuts

After the bodice is joined to the skirt, its shape becomes very important to the message of the costume. Modern—20th century—costume reflects human joints and is constructed, for the most part, to achieve easy movement. From 1700 to 1900 how it looked was much more important than how it worked. Theoretically, fashionable clothes did not have to work at all. You sat and looked pretty while others fetched and carried. Notice how constricting, but highly designed, these bodice cuts are. Of course, ladies got around total constriction with loose gowns and wrappers for "at home, undress" wear. If your goal in costuming is authenticity and believability, you will have to research and learn the cuts of costume...far more than I can show here.

We really can't have a discussion of stockings without considering garters. Until the introduction of elasticized threads, any leg covering that went above the calf was quite an awkward arrangement.

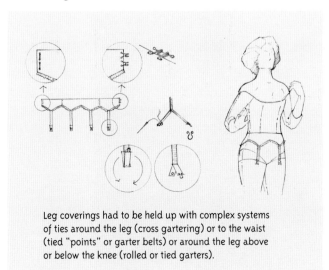

Leg coverings had to be held up with complex systems of ties around the leg (cross gartering) or to the waist (tied "points" or garter belts) or around the leg above or below the knee (rolled or tied garters).

Our elders remember clearly having to roll stocking tops around thick elastic bands that cut off circulation above or below the knee. Even children wore gartered stockings routinely. Others remember hooking stockings to garter belts and girdles while trying to keep back seams straight. When seamless panty hose came on the market in the late 1960's, women's liberation had truly arrived. Some men, however are still dealing with hooked calf garters.

Stockings themselves have been with us—especially in cold climates—for centuries. Earlier forms were more like leg warmers or tubes of woven wool or leather and fur, pulled up over the leg and tied in place. Knitted stockings of wool or silk have been with us since at least the 1600s. For most of the late medieval and Renaissance eras, stockings or hose were a very important visible part of the wardrobe for men. Generally, the hose consisted of two separate legs with no crotch connect that tied to the inner waistband of the doublet or upper garment. Separate covering for the crotch, a codpiece which operated like a trapdoor, was tied to the waist or built into the pants part depending on the style of the era. Trapdoor effects bring us to the "Union suit" or long underwear, a combination of stockings and body covering, which was an invention of the Victorian era.

Separately constructed stockings are always an effective touch; remember, people will look. Because of the availability of many different stocking materials of stretch fabric, some really nice details can be achieved in a few minutes of hand or machine sewing. Start by accumulating a collection of discarded stockings, colored tights, and hose from the household or thrift shop. Look for small clocks and argyle patterns. Look for sales on party hose at hosiery shops—there you can get fine gold and silver mesh as well as lacy and embroidered fashions. To keep scale in hand, use the top parts of panty hose or tights when you want a heavier look.

Any knit fabric or stocking material can be sewn on the machine. If binding under the machine foot is a problem, place a piece of tissue paper under the fabric, sew a straight seam, and remove tissue before turning. Start turn, place over toe and continue turning and rolling up the leg. Machine-sewing, however, will create a seam allowance that you might prefer not to have. Hand-sewing will eliminate that and, moreover, will make a seam that looks very much like a real stocking.

Note: For sculpted dolls, be sure to paint legs flesh color so that leg color showing through sheer stockings looks natural. Add texture by stippling or brushing a second color over the first.

■ Mary Jo Carpenter, *Flame,* 14 inches, Super Sculpey.
Photo by Mary Jo Carpenter.

■ Jeanie Bates, *Madame Marie-Rose,* 24 inches, cloth.
Photo by William S. Sullivan.

■ Antonette Cely, *Decisions, Decisions,*
16 inches, fabric.
Photo by Don B. Cely.

Hats, Caps, and Head Coverings

The Crowning Glory

Completing the figure on the top end, with headgear, serves a design function, sends a social or economic message, declares rank or creates a dramatic effect. Think of the mystery of a face hidden in a hood; think of the humor of a big floppy hat with feathers; or consider the startling effect of a wire contraption. Unless your figure is going to carry its message by hairstyle alone, you need to consider some sort of head wear. We can break headgear into three different categories by construction methods: molded or formed, stitched straw, and sewn cloth.

Materials

Before you start, here are the basic materials you need:

Buckram: Cotton gauze saturated with stiffener. When this is dampened and formed over a block it will dry to shape. It can also be sewn between layers of fabric for stiffening fabric hat brims.

Wire: 20-gauge galvanized will be adequate for typical doll sizes.

Thin, hollow metal tubing: This can be purchased where model-making supplies are sold. Wire ends are inserted into a small piece of tubing to make a wire brim frame or re-enforcement.

Fabric stiffener: Purchase in a fabric or craft shop. If not available, thinned white glue can be used—carefully.

Blocks: Traditionally, hats made of fiber—usually wool—have been steam molded over forms or "blocked." For sculpted figures you can use the head of the figure itself as a form (prior to painting and finishing it) or you can find a form that will work for the head size. In hat manufacture, blocking forms are usually made of wood, steel or very hard-packed canvas for shaping with steam. In the studio, we can simulate forms by using bottle caps, drinking glasses, salt and pepper shakers, Styrofoam balls or eggs, small bowls, or any hard item in a desired shape. Contemporary felt has a very low percentage of wool so you do not need to steam. Fabric stiffener will hold shapes quite nicely without steaming.

Straw: Braided or woven hat straw can sometimes be found in craft stores; however, you might find it too large in scale. Purchase old hats at a thrift shop, cut stitching, and pull into strips of braid.

1. Choose or make a form that will fit your figure.

2. If using Styrofoam balls, cover form (or head of figure) with plastic wrap so fabric does not stick to the foam.

3. Cut a square of felt and saturate it in fabric stiffener. Commercial stiffeners are available at craft stores or you can use a 50-50 mixture of white glue and water, or you can use laundry starch. The important thing is to fully saturate the material. Squeeze out excess liquid so fabric is damp, not soggy and dripping.

4. Drape material over form and secure with rubber band. Pull material and work under the rubber band so that the crown is free of wrinkles.

5. Trim brim material to desired shape and with fingers work out wrinkles until material is as smooth and flat as possible. Let dry. Remove from form, peel away plastic protection and trim to finish.

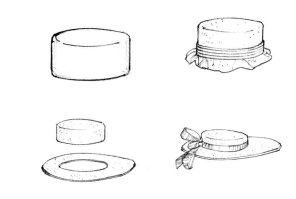

Hints

■ Crowns and complex brims can be formed separately and stitched together. This same process can be used with fabric stiffener or starch on cotton laces. You can do this same process using water-damped felt alone, although the result will be soft. However, crown interiors can be additionally re-inforced by painting on a coat of clear acrylic medium or white glue.

■ To make an oval-shaped form, cut a Styrofoam egg lengthwise and crush narrow end in slightly.

■ To make hats with a crown indent, cut and sew hat pieces together, saturate fabric, place on form so that top extends higher than form, use your fingers to set crease, and let dry.

■ To make hat with a rolled brim, cut crown as shown for tilt, sew on brim, saturate brim and shape with fingers. Pin, if necessary, to hold in place until dry. A prop bed for drying can also be made with crushed aluminum foil.

Sewn Forms

Hat bases or forms can be sewn of nylon/polyester buckram. Additional stiffening can be applied by using a machine zigzag stitch to sew wire around outside of brim or bottom of crown. The buckram base is then covered with flowers, feathers and/or fabric. Be aware feathers can be destroyed by insects. A shot of bug spray might help prevent this.

Stitched Forms

Braided straw, lace, or narrow trim may be stitched together in a coiled system. You may want to use a stiffener with softer materials.

The Straw Hat

Materials

Braided milliner's straw. Old straw hats may be cut apart into their original strips.

20-gauge wire (optional)

Starting from the center, stitch braid into a circle until it is as big as the desired crown size. Decide how high you want the crown. Sew until band reaches desired height. Begin brim by stitching braid at right angles to the band. Sew until desired brim width is achieved. Strips are extended outward by layering and tapering ends of successive rows. If needed, 20-gauge wire may be stitched into last row of brim to add stiffening.

Hints

Make a smooth wire join by inserting wire ends into hollow metal tubing. Crush tubing against wire with pliers to hold. Metal tubing maybe purchased at model makers' supply shops.

■ Margaret Finch and Marta Finch-Kozlosky, *Eglisia,* 14 inches, cloth, Fimo. Photo by Charles Kozlosky.

The "Skimmer"

A "skimmer" is a hat with no crown and band. It is just a circle of straw, felt, or fabric, with a circle cut out of the middle. You might want to try cutting a circle of net for a base and stitching braid or lace around it.

The "Bucket Hat"

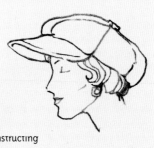

This is the basic shape for the typical toque hat worn in the 1920s and 1950s. From soft foam rubber cut rounded shape. Hollow out interior to fit head. Cover with lightweight silk, chiffon or organdy. Add a layer of hat netting, or glue on silk flowers or stitch on decorative fibers. Foam balls that are used inside yarn balls make excellent cloche forms.

The "Newsboy Cap"

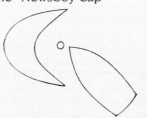

Here are the basic patterns for constructing a cloth cap.

The "Mob Cap"

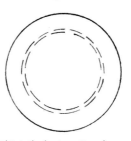

This is the basic pattern for constructing a mob cap. Wonderful variations can be made using wider ribbon bands and falling laces.

The Helmet or Hard Hat

Cover head with plastic wrap and model form over it with paper clay.

Turban

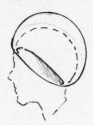

Mold a form of dampened buckram or stiffener-saturated fabric over head shape. Cover crown shape with fabric. Let it wrinkle as you bring ends to underside of form. Stitch to secure. Take two or three fabrics and one or two decorative trims and stitch around form, twisting at back, front and sides as you go. Add jewel and decorative feathers

Bonnet: *Cardboard Covered*

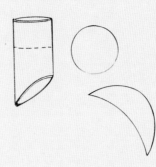

Cut or construct hat band from cardboard. Cover with fabric leaving 1/4-inch over each edge.

Insert crown into band and hand-stitch together. Cut brim of cardboard and use it as a pattern to cut cover fabric.

Machine stitch outer edge of brim and insert cardboard brim. Turn under ends and stitch to band. Cover stitched areas with small decorative trim, add flowers and ribbons.

The Tip-Tilted Hat

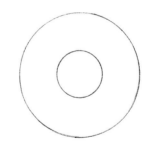

Hats that have a peek-a-boo look are held in place by a prop. Essentially they are a brim inserted onto a molded head form. The brim is adjusted to the desired angle and stitched to the head form.

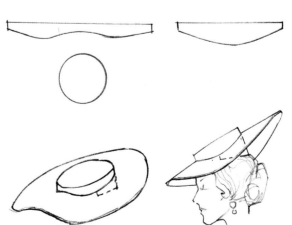

Shoes

Getting to the Bottom of It

The stuffed cloth doll provides groundwork for a number of shoe treatments. You can embroider the outline and fill it in with decorative stitches. You can paint it or you can create the shoe as a separate pattern piece and sew it as one with the leg, using a different fabric. Anything you can do to embellish cloth—from bubble paint to machine embroidery—can be done to simulate a shoe on a stuffed doll. However, with a stuffed doll, it will be important to be sure your total design look in finish treatments is carried through in the feet.

In the sculpted doll, it is often more important to the design to have the shoe be realistic and in conformance to the style of the costume era. An impressive shoe will always get points with the viewer. As with cloth, you can model the shoe in the same material as the leg. Depending on your design look, when you work with air drying or oven curing clays, the buckles, eyelets, hooks, and laces of other materials can be applied during the modeling.

Most artists like to make the shoe so that it gives the impression of having been put on. To do that well, you must acquire a good understanding of how "people" shoes are made.

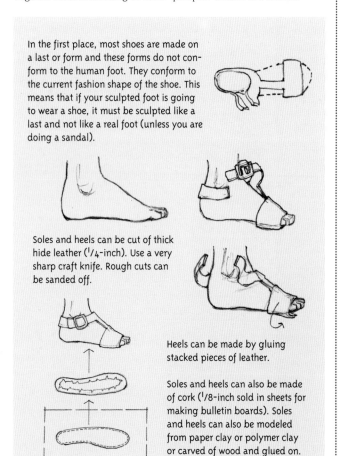

In the first place, most shoes are made on a last or form and these forms do not conform to the human foot. They conform to the current fashion shape of the shoe. This means that if your sculpted foot is going to wear a shoe, it must be sculpted like a last and not like a real foot (unless you are doing a sandal).

Soles and heels can be cut of thick hide leather (1/4-inch). Use a very sharp craft knife. Rough cuts can be sanded off.

Heels can be made by gluing stacked pieces of leather.

Soles and heels can also be made of cork (1/8-inch sold in sheets for making bulletin boards). Soles and heels can also be modeled from paper clay or polymer clay or carved of wood and glued on.

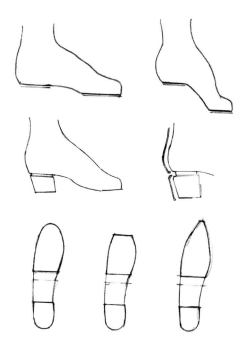

Most shoes are variations of an open sandal (Roman matron or modern high heel), the plain flat slipper, the pump which is simply a heeled slipper, the laced boot, and the slip-on boot.

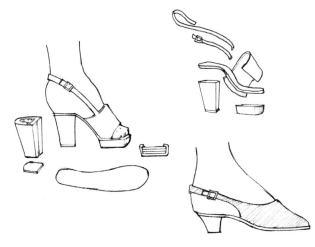

■ Antonette Cely, *Decisions, Decisions* detail, 16 inches, fabric.
Photo by Don B. Cely.

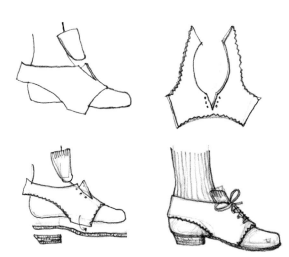

Most shoes consist of an upper—the part that fits the foot top and the sole or the part we walk on, an inner sole, and the heel. Your doll shoe will need all four parts.

Authenticity is a must in historical costume and familiarity with small details helps underscore the impression. Did you know that shoes were not made specifically for right and left feet until they were manufactured? Did you know that patens—a high wooden slip-ons—were used by both men and women for outdoor wear for several centuries? Did you know that wooden shoes were worn, and still are worn, by farmers in many countries?

If cardboard is used for soles and heels, it should be covered with leather or leather looking fabric. Heavy bodied paint or liquid latex applied by dipping or by brush can simulate a rubber soled tennis shoe sole. Imagine how you would make a golf or baseball shoe with cleats?

■ Deborah Spanton, *Rooster Man,* 16 inches, cloth and wire. Photo by Bill Bachhuber.

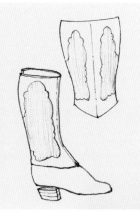

■ Chris Chomick and Peter Meder, *Christopher Pete on Vacation,* 21 inches, Super Sculpey. Leather boots made by Peter Meder. Photo by Chris Chomick.

■ Martha Boers and Marianne Reitsma, *Lakon Nai*,
  18 inches, polymer clay.
  Photo by Chris Crossley.

CHAPTER FIVE

Embellishments

Considerations

With embellishment, what you do has to work with and be seen as seamlessly integral with the piece. Embellishment is not a matter of adding trim, showing off a technique or "sticking things on top." Successful embellishment comes from within the design concept, with the aim of enriching the visual experience.

Embellishment is not limited to contemporary or historical costume figures. Many of us incorporate elements of the folk and ethnic costume as well as the abstract in our work. Let's take a look at how we might approach these types when we think about design.

Folk Costume

Much of folk and fairytale costume can be defined as contemporary fashion adapted to country or local materials and embellishment preferences. Or, it can evolve from people's particular needs and what materials are available.

A good example of ethnic costume might be the evolution of the Manchu coat from the outline of an animal hide.

The design, which is split to wear for horseback riding, has narrowed sleeves with cuffs to protect hands in rain or snow, and which can be lined in fur. Another example of ethnic clothing evolves from the straight length of woven fabric designed for clothing that can be folded flat with minimal wrinkling.

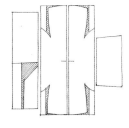

The Han Chinese dress with its pleated skirts is typical of a style evolved in a culture where woven goods were available and people did not routinely conduct life on horseback. A kimono, a sari, or a caftan are good examples of flat fold design.

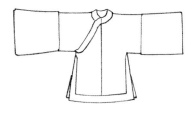

■ (Above) Jaine Lamb, *Sky Woman* detail, 19 inches, Cernit. Photo by Jaine Lamb.

■ Richard and Jody Creager, *Follow the Leader*, 12 inches, Super Sculpey. Photo by Richard Creager.

■ June Goodnow, *Wolf Robe of the Cheyenne,*
14 inches, polymer clay. Photo by Brian Schul.

Hints

The major difficulty with choosing a flat, robe-like ethnic costume is working with large, shapeless, bland expanses of material. For the doll costumer, ethnic styles can go on any type and you can mix and match elements for added effect. Use the flat fold styles to show off your patterned and woven fabrics. Use the following to help make the figure more interesting: *First,* be sure the figure has a good body with shoulders, hips, waist and bust. Most simple clothing will and should flow over and reflect these major body parts. *Second,* choose a pose that might allow you to add some draping that will accentuate the body beneath the clothing. For instance, a seated pose will allow you to show wrinkles at the hip and perhaps the top of the thigh, and it also allows you to show a foot in sandals or boots. *Third,* consider stiffening or wiring skirts and full sleeves to show motion.

■ Jaine Lamb, *Dancing Doe,* 10 inches, seated, Cernit.
Photo by W. Donald Smith.

■ June Goodnow, *Eskimos Dancing,*
19 inches, polymer clay.
Photo by Brian Schul.

■ Marilynn Huston, *Guinevere,* 18 inches, Super Sculpey.
Photo by Eileen Richmond.

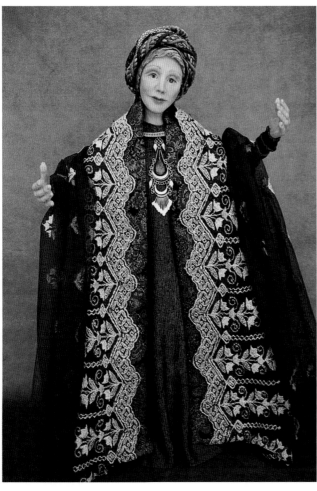

■ Marilynn Huston, *Queen Esther,* 18 inches, Super Sculpey.
Photo by Eileen Richmond.

■ Ruth Landis, *Garden Angel,*
16 inches, cloth.
Photo by Ruth Landis.

The Abstract

The naked figure or the figure in its basic costume becomes the basic for any number of embellishment techniques which will enhance the message of the piece. Most of us have an idea of what these will be when we identify the initial idea. Most of us can't wait to get to that part...and a whole lot of us have learned some highly skilled crafts in order to complete this kind of a piece.

In contemporary figure making, the figure itself often begins the statement. A cloth body can be made of a solid, non-flesh color or print. That actual body can be finished with quilting, embroidery, printing, stamping, or painting.

Unless your idea is to convey a real-world ethnic body embellishment such as tattooing or body painting, in most cases when the figure itself becomes the ground, the result will fall into the category of absurd or abstract. Realistic historical or contemporary clothing involves useful clothing that people can work and keep warm in and clothing made from materials available to a particular society. When you get to the abstract or absurd, we can use these elements, but we can slide out of the conventional boxes. Absurd costumes don't have to look like a person can put them on; the idea is to show shapes and mixes of material that underscore the comic or odd. The message is something like: This is an unusual character who will not reflect the world as we know it. Animal personification figures or figures that use animal elements are basically absurd. Animals don't wear top hats. There is no such thing as a lady with a fish tail in the real world. This means you have all kinds of freedom to express these kinds of ideas. The abstract figure is usually made to convey a design message such as "Here is a human in an unusual shape"—perhaps a star or perhaps a set of circular shapes. Comic and cartooned figures are essentially abstracts. They signal something different is going on because of their non-human body shapes.

Does this make it "no-holds-barred-anything-goes?" No, indeed. Working with the abstract means that the designer—with only her imagination and design skill—must put together shapes, textures, and technical elements thoughtfully and effectively, all by herself. As opposed to contemporary or historical costume, there is no no-fail recipe for making an abstract piece. What I can tell you is to be always aware of your design and the elements of balance and proportion, line and texture when you render your idea.

The following pages provide a general survey of embellishment techniques most commonly used by figure artists and some easy steps to access them. For each one—sewing, embroidery, machine work, weaving, beading, printing, dyeing, or painting—you will be able to find one or more books that thoroughly introduce you to the details of execution. Use your library to research the ones you like. Take classes if you can, or experiment in your kitchen or sewing room until you can make them a natural part of your embellishment repertoire.

■ Barbara Morrison, *Acteon Reflecting on His Past*, 12 inches, polymer clay, mixed media. Photo by Geoff Sutton.

■ (Left and above) Anne Mayer Meier and Gabrielle Cyr, *The Friendship Spirit Dolls,* 16 inches, fabric. Photo by Jerry White.

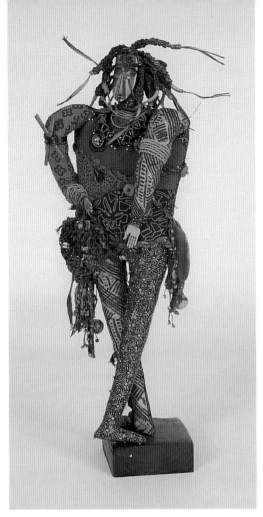

■ Anne Mayer Meier, *Man and Woman*,
12 inches, fabric, clay.
Photo by Jerry White.

■ Pamela Armas, *The Ancient One*,
22 inches, fabric with bone face.
Photo by Charles Lundy.

■ Sandra Feingold, *Silent Wisdom*,
23 inches, cloth, leather and gourd.
Photo by Sandra Feingold.

■ Martha Ann Dudley, *Jamaka*,
21 inches, fabric.
Photo by Steve Rucker.

Custom Fabrics and Trims

Picture the world of arts and crafts. Think about how the skills and materials of the art of painting pictures are developed out of the work itself. All the things a painter wants to know relate to achieving a picture with brushes, canvas or paint. All the potter wants to know is related to building clay, firing and glazing. The painter doesn't use ceramic glaze nor does the potter use watercolor. The doll maker, however, is likely to know quite a bit about both ceramics and painting. The doll maker is a sculptor in the purest sense. He takes any raw material and any technique he needs—from painting, weaving, dyeing, ceramics, and every one of the needle and fiber arts—and applies it to finishing his figure. The more he knows, the more he can draw from.

Most of us who make figures have quite a battery of skills and they are so integral to our work, we don't even think about them as separate fields. We may not always be masters of each one, but we learn them well enough to do what needs to be done for our piece.

What follows is a survey of some of the fiber and needle work skills doll makers today are using in their work....just a brief outline, an easy approach or two, and some ideas which I hope will encourage you to explore further on your own. If something strikes your fancy, make time for reading and research and take time for classes and experimentation.

■ Mary Ellen Frank, *Walter Soboleff,* 14 inches, wood and cloth. Photo by Mary Ellen Frank.

■ Mary Ellen Frank, *Three Generations,* 14 inches, hand carved Alaska Paper Birch, cloth body. Photos by Mailynn Holmes.

■ Ethel Loh Strickarz, *Raven,* 21 inches, stone clay. Photo by Ethel Loh Strickarz.

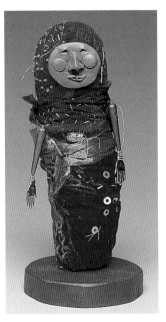

■ Priscilla McGarry, *My Friend,*
9 inches, cloth over wire.
Photo by Althea Church.

■ Tracy Page Stillwell,
Red Pod, 17 inches, cloth.
Photo by David Carras.

■ Melinda Small Paterson, *Bov Dearg,*
6 inches, polymer clay.
Photo by Melinda Small Paterson.

■ Bronwyn Hayes, *Gnome,*
52 cm, cloth.
Photo by Bronwyn Hayes.

■ Alinda Boyce-Franklin, *Spirit Song
of the Moon,* 26 inches, cloth.
Photo by Alinda Boyce-Franklin.

Custom Work

Sometimes no fabric or trim in the world exists to get the effect you want. What to do? Make your own.

Painting

Did you paint the doll's body? Why not paint the doll's clothing? See what Jan Collins-Langford has done in creating aprons for her cloth dolls. Woven fabrics tempt us in this direction because they look like canvas, but look, Maggie Iacono has successfully mastered painting on felt.

For painting on fabric about anything goes. You do have to remember that if you use oil paints, they will need to be painted on a solid ground—any exposed fabric can show oil bleed or puddling. Chemicals in oil paints applied directly can degrade fabric over time. Watercolors or highly thinned acrylics can bleed as well. On the other hand, bleeding or puddling can be used for impressionistic effects. If you want to use oils or achieve sharp edges, prime your fabric with a layer of gesso. Don't paint until gesso is thoroughly dry. Also note that alkyd oil paints dry somewhat faster. Work with your materials, not against them. For instance, if you want to apply color to a fuzzy surface, consider stamping rather than brushwork. Or, consider outlining a painted area with hand- or machine-embroidery. Combined effects can be striking.

Under the heading of "Weird Stuff—you never know what might be good," several fabric paints are available that do things like puff or bubble, or even give a fuzzy look. You can get hot glue in any number of colors and some with glitter...shoot it onto fabric and see what you get.

■ Christine Shively, *Serenity,* 16 inches, fabric, beads, silk. Photo by Christine Shively.

■ Annie Wahl, *The Four Sister Queens,* 11 inches, Super Sculpey, hand painted costumes. Photo by W. Donald Smith.

■ Dawn Kinsey, *Tingadae,* 9 inches,
dyed silk and paper clay.
Photo by Dawn Kinsey.

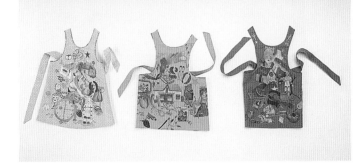

■ Jan Collins-Langford, *Aprons for Dot, Sparkle, and Fleck,* each 22$^1/_4$ inches,
hand-painted cotton. Photo by Geoff Carr.

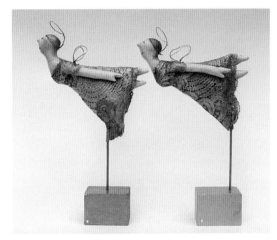

■ Willemijn van der Spiegel, *Zweefjes,* 20 cm,
impregnated, painted fabric.
Photo by Ad van den Brink.

■ Deb Shattill, *Lute Player,*
22 inches, fabric and beads.
Photo by Deb Shattil.

■ Deb Shattil, *Golden Nude,*
11 inches, cloth.
Photo by Deb Shattil.

■ Pamela Cowart-Rickman, *In Memoria*, 28 inches, fabric, hand painted.
Photo by Jerry Anthony.

Stencils and Stamps

Manufactured prints are stamped (printed) or stenciled. You can do that. You might have done it already.

You could make stamped designs with commercially available stamps or stencils which might be fun for doing words, names or messages. If you use a purchased stamp or stencil, you should give copyright credit to the producer somewhere on your piece. In most cases, you will probably find it more satisfactory to your original design scheme to make up your own designs.

Making Your Own Stamps

Use a potato cut in half or pink pencil eraser for small designs. For larger designs, you can use sponges or purchase linoleum print blocks ready to cut at a craft or art supplier. Doll makers often solve scale problems when very tiny prints are needed by making their own stamps cut from a pencil eraser. Draw a simple design such as a flower on the eraser or potato. Cut out design at least $1/8$-inch deep with sharp craft knife. For multiple colors make separate stamps for each color. Be sure to key the second stamp so designs do not overlap.

Making Your Own Stencils

Plastic sheets with pre-cut designs or plain for cutting your own can be purchased in craft stores. If those aren't available, you can do it yourself.

First, prepare cotton by washing to remove any sizing. Use fabric paints or acrylics. Make a stencil by drawing your design on a piece of stiff paper such as an index card or file folder. Melt household paraffin (use a double boiler); and with an old brush, paint both sides of the stencil paper with a thin coat of paraffin. This will keep paint from soaking into the paper. Now, cut the design you drew on the stencil paper with sharp craft knife. Pin or tape fabric tightly to a magazine. Tape the stencil over the fabric and paint design, moving brush from cut edge of stencil to inside. This makes the edge of the design darker and more outlined. If you are doing a multiple stencil, start with the smallest element—such as the center of a flower—and follow with petals and then leaves. If you are making a large repeated design, change magazine underlayment before doing the next section.

When you use stamps or stencils, you can make the design a little more interesting by hand painting small details with a brush.

■ Sara Austin, *Lucy #1 as Vasalisa*, 16 inches, fabric, photo transfers, embroidery.
Photo by Sara Austin.

Embossing

Velvet stamping—ironing velvet over a raised surface—will crush the pile, and if the raised surface has a design, you will achieve an effect very much like cut velvet. For this you need a commercial rubber stamp with a fairly simple bold design, or any raised design in a hard material. Use silk velvet and place it pile side down on the stamp or design surface, lower iron straight down and hold a few seconds. Look around, you could probably make sharp impressions by ironing your velvet over pieces of jewelry. What about metal cookie cutters? *Be sure the heat of the iron will not melt the item used for embossing.*

Printing

Traditionally, the home craftsman has printed fabric with the silk screen process or, if adventuresome, made a photographic sun exposure on fabric. Computers, photocopiers, and scanners give us a whole range of new possibilities to do at home. Printing on fabric can also be done in the copy shop from your design, photo or computer disk with larger color photocopiers. Jean Ray Laury's book, *Imagery on Fabric* details these and a number of other methods. Here are two that I have used.

■ (Below) Sara Austin, *Angela #3 with Sumo Wrestlers,* 16 inches, fabric, heat design transfers and machine appliqué. Photo by Sara Austin.

■ (Right) Sara Austin, *Baby Girl Inuit,* 12 inches, fabric. Photo by Sara Austin.

Spoon Print

A really easy way to begin photo transfer came from Australia via Judith Baker Montano, silk ribbon embroiderer. To do this you need natural fabric (silk, cotton, linen), a photocopy made with toner, paint thinner or turpentine, a spoon and an ink blotter. Put your fabric on the blotter, lay photocopy face down on the fabric, use a cotton ball to rub back of photocopy with thinner until transparent (don't over-soak or print will be runny). Then, rub the spoon on the photocopy to press image into the fabric. That's it. Paint thinner and turpentine are flammable. Don't use around flame, and make sure you work in a well-ventilated area.

Direct

Iron a piece of cotton fabric to the waxed side of a piece of freezer paper. Make sure you have a complete uniform bond. Trim edges to fit standard $8^1/_2$ x 11" or 11 x 14" computer printer tray sizes. Be exact in your measurement. Create your design on the computer. Remember, clip art is often copyrighted, so make up your own design with print fonts and/or shapes. Or, if you have a scanner, designs and photographs may be used. Add color. Load the paper-backed fabric and print. Expect the result to be not quite as sharp as a paper print. If your printer is an ink jet, the ink will not be waterproof.

Printer Transfer

Office suppliers carry special packs of paper that can be used with computer-generated or scanned images to make iron-on transfers.

■ Margi Hennen, *Catherine Walks Her Spotted Cod,*
10 inches, dye painting, photo transfer, stamping.
Photo by Warren Dodgson.

Dyeing

Most doll makers don't mind a little mess and are often happiest when making one. I made my first dye mess at the age of nine experimenting with my mother's laundry blueing and starch. Many beginner doll makers are very concerned with being exactly correct about products. Relax, use your imagination. Many of the things that you can use can be found in the grocery store or around your house.

Tea dyeing is most often used by doll makers to tone down a bright solid or print fabric and bring the color into better scale for the figure. This is a simple matter of making a bowl of tea and dipping your fabric in it until it is the shade you want. You can also use coffee, but the results will be more brown. Kool-Aid and food coloring can also be used if you want colors and just about anything that will stain your clothes or carpet—soft drinks, catsup, berry juice, etc. See weaving and dyeing references for colors and formulae, if you like the idea of experimenting with plant materials from your yard. The fabric should be natural—cotton, wool, silk, or linen, as polyester fibers will not hold dye without pre-treatments.

Craft and fiber/yarn shops will usually carry starter kits of dyes. Patti Culea achieves her colorful pieces with protein-based dyes, and many dollmakers have followed her example. Surface designer Yvonne Porcella (below) has done several books dealing with color in fabric and dye. You can scrunch, tie, or use a wax resist, sponges, eye droppers, spray misters and paint brushes for varying patterns. Line up your dye jars and tint to your heart's content. By the way, you can also dye bits of old cotton lace or silk ribbon for great trim effects.

Be sure to protect surfaces with plastic and use a press cloth to protect your iron when dyeing or painting.

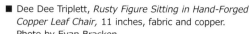

■ Dee Dee Triplett, *Rusty Figure Sitting in Hand-Forged Copper Leaf Chair,* 11 inches, fabric and copper. Photo by Evan Bracken.

■ Yvonne Porcella, *Three Muses—Aee, Bee and Cee,*
14 inches, handpainted cotton and silk.
Photo by Sharon Risedorph.

Burning

A quick way to keep the edges on a synthetic material from fraying is to hold it over a flame. Hold high enough so that the edges melt but do not brown. Natural fibers such as silk, cotton and wool will singe, turn black, and crumble when held to a flame. Holding fabric over a flame high enough just to melt it makes interesting effects. Use smokeless candles or the clear flame of an alcohol lamp. Nancy Walters (below) used a heat gun to burn out interesting lace-like patterns in fabric. Be careful—work in a cleared area and keep a fire extinguisher nearby if you try burning techniques.

Machine Work

You probably paid a great deal for the sewing machine with a memory that makes a hundred different stitches. Are you using them? To get your money's worth, think about creating your own machine-embroidered designs. One artist routinely applies rows of various stitch patterns instead of sewn-on trim. This makes her doll's clothes look correctly scaled and, of course, reduces bulk. Want a small gold embroidered print for a small figure's vest? Use the fancier stitches and metallic threads to create it. Use the memory function to write the doll's name on her petticoats, or your name on a cloth tag to sew on the petticoat. Your sewing machine might be the source of all your trimming needs.

■ Ruth Landis, *Mistress Firefly,* 16 inches, cloth. Photo by Ruth Landis.

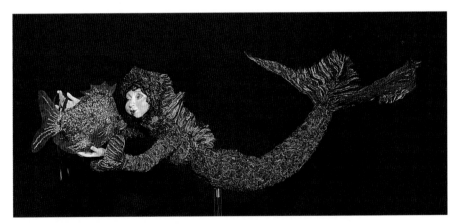

■ Nancy Walters, *Pisces,* 10 inches, air-drying clay, embellished with beading and machine embroidery over candled polyester chiffon fabric. Photo by Nancy Walters.

■ Julie McCullough, *Even Mother Earth Has Her Ups and Downs,* 30 inches, quilted fabrics. Photo by John Nollendorf.

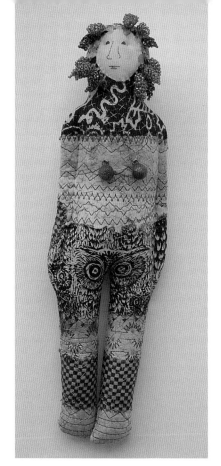

■ Margi Hennen, *3 Stages of Woman #2,* 12 inches, piecing, hand and machine embroidery, paint beading. Photo by Warren Dodgson.

■ Dee Dee Triplett, *Dandelion Dance,* 23 inches, cloth over wire, silk, cotton, and paper photo. Photo by Evan Bracken.

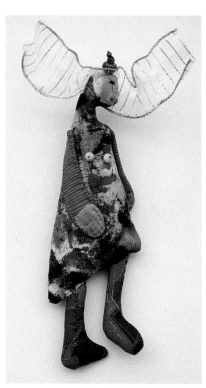

■ Margi Hennen, *Rowena,* 12 inches, fabric with dye, painting, stencil and stamping. Photo by Warren Dodgson.

■ Rita Carl, *Melody—Angel of Song,* 22 inches, cloth. Photo by Douglas Beck.

Handwork

There is no end to what you can do with your needle and thread to shape fabric in interesting ways. And when you have done that, you can use embroidery techniques, silk ribbon designs, knitting and crochet stitches to embellish further.

Needlework and Fabric Manipulation

There are many ways to manipulate fabric. Colette Wolff's book, *Fabric Manipulation*, is a treasure house of ideas for the doll maker.

Ribbon Flower

Since we are concerned with solving costume problems in terms of fabric bulk reduction, pleats are a method of manipulation that we need to look at closely. Most of us think of pleats as folds in fabric that are sewn across the top or at right angles to the fold. The cartridge pleat is a useful variation that deserves to be considered.

Five Petal Flower

Yo-Yo Flower

Scallop Flower

Pouf Flower

■ Bonnie Hoover, *Mademoiselle Babette,* 16 inches, *Fiona The Flower Fairy,* 16 inches, and *Griselda,* 18 inches.
The cloth costumes on these dolls were embellished by the artist with variation of traditional fabric techniques such as covered buttons and yo-yos.
Photos of Bonnie Hoover's dolls and details by Sandra Hoover.

Cartridge Pleats

A cartridge pleat (think of rows of holders sewn on a belt for holding ammunition) is a pleat where both sides of the fold are sewn at right angles to the base fabric. A good way to understand cartridge pleats is to look at the construction of an Elizabethan ruff.

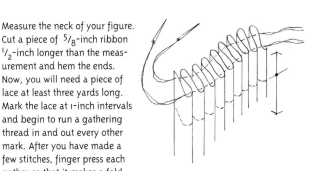

Measure the neck of your figure. Cut a piece of $5/8$-inch ribbon $1/2$-inch longer than the measurement and hem the ends. Now, you will need a piece of lace at least three yards long. Mark the lace at 1-inch intervals and begin to run a gathering thread in and out every other mark. After you have made a few stitches, finger press each gather so that it makes a fold. Take a second threaded needle and catch the point of each fold. Continue until you have a length of folded pleats.

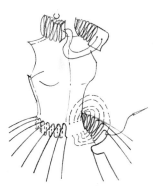

Stitch each fold to the neckband. Attach to costume. If you have a pleater you can press the pleats instead of marking the lace or fabric.

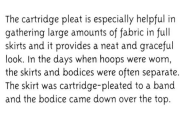

The cartridge pleat is especially helpful in gathering large amounts of fabric in full skirts and it provides a neat and graceful look. In the days when hoops were worn, the skirts and bodices were often separate. The skirt was cartridge-pleated to a band and the bodice came down over the top.

Mademoiselle Babette

Fiona

Griselda

The Pleater

Mechanical pleaters can be purchased (look in sewing magazines); however, doll maker's needs might not justify the expense or the space. You can make a flat-fold pleater for yourself. The principle is that rods are held by equally spaced nails opposite each other on a board. The fabric is laid, a rod is placed and the fabric is folded back over the rod and another rod is placed. After the fabric has been laid, it is ironed to hold the pleats so your board needs to be a bit wider than the width of your iron. It helps to lay fabric wrong side up and, after pressing, tape the pleats so they will hold in place until you have machine sewn them to secure.

Constructing a pleater

With a hammer, nails, and a board, measure spacing of $1/4$-inch and set a nail on either side. Nailing neatly is not easy. You can get the same effect with any sort of grid or mesh. For instance, use a folded piece of fine wire screen or mesh, a strip of plastic or heavy cardboard with holes punched, or a piece of electrical circuit board. Metal rods can be purchased at a shop where model railroad materials are sold.

Rotary Cutters

Almost every artist tried to use the decorative paper scissors on fabric—and found they didn't work very well. However, you can purchase rotary cutters with 6 or 8 different patterned blades. Use iron-on fusible interfacing if you want both sides to show fabric or one-sided fusible fabric if you need to keep woven edges from fraying.

■ Heather Maciak, *Three Vests and a Jacket.*
Pieced and embroidered cloth.
Photo by Heather Maciak.

■ Heather Maciak, *Amelia and Eloise,* 10 inches,
porcelain, ball-jointed bodies.
Photo by Heather Maciak.

■ Kathryn Belzer, *Taos Diva,* 12 inches, cloth.
Photo by Gary Castle.

Weaving

Contemporary doll makers often employ weaving as part of their work. A loom for a small piece can be made with a piece of cardboard and some popsicle sticks. Barbara Evans and her doll making colleagues have made some lovely pieces by weaving assorted fancy yarns and fibers together in one piece.

Pin Weaving

Pin weaving can be done directly on the figure. Place pins where you want the weaving to be. Loop yarn around pins to form the warp. Use a tapestry needle or ribbon needle to weave with ribbons or fibers or a combination.

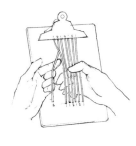

Needle Lace

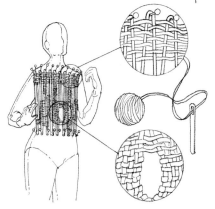

With a long thread on the needle, create your own abstract patterns by varying the strands you pick up. Make it more interesting by adding another layer on top. You can do this on the cardboard loom or directly on the figure. This is a great way to embellish an abstract fabric figure.

■ Annie Wylde-Beem, *Pinky*, 5 inches, embroidery thread, beads. Photo by Annie Wylde-Beem.

Finger Lace

Some interesting effects can be achieved by splitting the strands, weaving each group separately for a space and then re-joining the group. This makes a slashed or slotted look similar to the needle lace. Experiment with your own patterns.

Finger Weaving

Doll makers often use finger weaving to create belts or special effects on costumes. Finger weaving looks difficult, but when you have gotten the hang of it, you will say, "Oh, this is easy." When you start for the first time, hold these ideas in your head. One: there is no loom, your hands function as both loom and weaver. Two: Each warp thread (long, vertical) will take its turn being a weft (diagonal cross warp) thread.

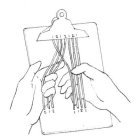

Practice this way: Cut 20 pieces of yarn about 15 inches long. Lay close together in a row and secure ends with a binder clip or by taping securely to a table edge. This is the warp. Pick up strands in one hand. With the other hand, take the end strand nearest your free hand. With your fingers, pass this strand over and under until it gets to the other side of the stands.

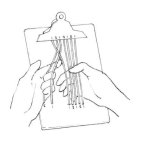
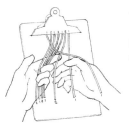

The hand with the single strand will lead it. The fingers of the hand holding the group will lay each strand over or under it.

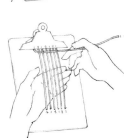

After all the threads have been passed, the work will have been transferred from one hand to the other.

Pass the group back to the hand that originally held them. Then, take the next strand next to your free hand, and pass it over and under across the warp. This strand will weave in the first one that went across. Continue using the outside strand on one side to pass. When it gets to the far side, it bends down and becomes a warp strand again.

It will look messy for the first few rows, but give it a chance. Because you are using the warp thread from one side to weave with on each row, the weaving will tend to work sideways as you add rows. The piece will begin to have a diagonal look. After a few rows have been done, you can push the work to straighten it out. It will take at least a few rows to get a pattern going, and more than one attempt to pick up a rhythm. This is something to try when you can be quiet by yourself. When you have mastered the rhythm of this method, try weaving back and forth.

Felt

Felting is a process of making fabric without weaving or spinning. Legend has it that felt was the result of camel drivers putting camel hair into their shoes and walking it into a mat; but as hair does not felt, it seems more likely that felt was the result of nomads using sheepskins as horse blankets or shoe liners. Technically, heat causes barbs in wool fibers to open, and pressure causes breakdown and oozing of cell structure of the fibers between barbs which create a mat. Additional heat and pressure cause the matted fibers to shrink. Hair and synthetic fibers can be added to fibers being felted, but they themselves do not felt.

Method I

The traditional way. You need natural wool fibers—cleaned of oils and animal debris from the sheep or goat. The fibers are then carded or combed so that they lie straight and parallel. Hand carded puffs or lengths of drum carded wool which look like hair ropes can be purchased through weaving and spinning suppliers. Many doll makers have the rope type in their hair stash. Choose wool with fibers that are about an inch in length. You can make felt from carded lengths as follows:

1. Lay out a piece of cotton fabric that is about 10 x 20 inches. Pull lengths of wool fibers from puffs or strands and lay them on one half of the fabric. Lay in thin layers and place each layer at a right angle to the one below. Build layers until you have a "cloud" of at least five or six layers. Fold fabric end over and hand baste to make closed package.

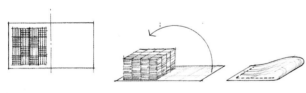

2. Sprinkle package with hot water and a tiny dab of liquid soap and press water through it until thoroughly soaked. Use rubber gloves. When soaked, place package on wooden board over sink. Alternately add hot water from kettle or tap and roll package with rolling pin. Do this for 15 minutes. This creates a hardened mat.

3. Open package and gently peel fiber mat away from cotton. Again, on the board, sprinkle hot water on mat and roll with rolling pin. Roll and sprinkle alternately keeping water hot. The pressure of the rolling action and the hot water causes the fibers to shrink and lock.

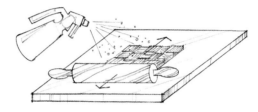

You can continue this for 20 minutes to an hour (breaks are OK) until fibers don't move when rubbed. Remember that the piece will be fuzzy and it will be much thicker than commercially processed felt. You can make nifty felt balls by rolling leftover fibers between your palms with hot water, and a tiny (pinhead size) dab of liquid soap.

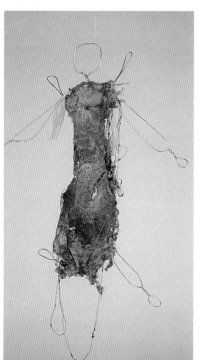

■ Susanna Oroyan, *Lintangel,* 15 inches wire and dryer lint felt. Lint was shaped by drying the piece over a crumpled foil form. Photo by W. Donald Smith.

■ Jan Clements, *Autumn,* 53 cm. Natural fibers are felted and built-up to produce a sculptural head. Photo by Jan Clements.

Method II

Yes, dryer lint is an acceptable doll making material. You can use it for hair or in any place it works with the design idea; primarily, it is used to make felt. Here's how:

Let the dryer lint trap collect lint to a thickness of about an inch. Carefully peel the lint away. You will notice the lint layers itself in colors depending on what you have dried. You can try to control color results by drying colored fluffy rugs, stuffed toys or sweatshirts. If you have pets or wash a feather pillow, or facial tissue, you will get some interesting effects in your lint.

On a large, flat surface, lay a piece of kitchen aluminum foil longer than your dryer lint piece. Over the foil place a piece of kitchen plastic wrap. In a bowl mix liquid fabric stiffener and water in equal parts. Pour about two tablespoons over plastic wrap. Lay dryer lint over plastic and foil. Sprinkle more liquid mixture over lint and cover with a second piece of plastic wrap. Use a rolling pin to spread and thoroughly saturate. This process might tear or distort lint. That's OK. Take advantage of the forms that appear. You can make folds or wrinkles in the foil to contour piece and/or give it dimension. When you have a pleasing shape, let dry. Drying can be accelerated by using a fan, portable heater or by putting in the oven with the door open and the temperature set at warm. When dry, lint will be quite stiff, like heavy paper, and you can carefully peel away plastic wrap and foil.

Embellish either type of felt with machine, silk or yarn embroidery. Use tissue paper backing when machine sewing.

- (Right) Susanna Oroyan, *The Elemental Empress,*
  20 inches, paper clay figure, costume panel of dryer lint.
  Photo by W. Don Smith.

- Nancy Cronin, *The Wisdom Women,* 12 inches, Super
  Sculpey and made wool felt. Felt has been stitched and
  needle sculpted to cone shaped thread spool to form the body.
  Photo by Nancy Cronin.

- Barbara Carleton Evans, *The Shepherd and his Lamb,*
  8 inches, handmade felt and found materials.
  Photo by Randall Encinas.

Beadwork

Beadwork can be the whole finish of a figure, or its entire costume, or a rich textural highlight. Beadwork can be purchased or hand done. Doing it yourself goes surprisingly faster than you might think and it can be addictive... just another and another. Many doll makers carry beading projects as easy pick-up handwork to do while chatting or traveling.

We tend to think of beaded costumes as a Native American tradition, but beading is found in any number of cultures done with many different types of beads—bone, shell, glass—anything one can drill a hole in that a needle can pass through. You can make your own. Here is how you can make your own from paper scraps.

Cut a triangle of paper (brightly colored magazine pages are good to use). Apply glue to back side of paper and roll over a darning needle. If you like, paint on a clear gloss finish. You can do this with squares and rectangles of paper as well.

The following basics can get you started...and maybe finished with an original project. Try some free-form without a pattern. If you need specific design, you will need to make a pattern on grid paper for reference.

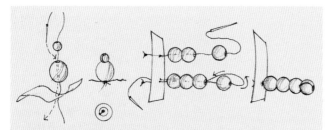

Single sets/double back stitch—This makes a pleasing all-over ground. You can also use the double back to end a string or in making a fringe.

Single stitch—here each bead is separately stitched onto the fabric.

Multiple—Any number of beads can be threaded on the needle, laid in place and stitched into place at intervals.

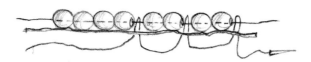

Couching— A string may be secured by stitching down the stringing thread between each bead or at intervals.

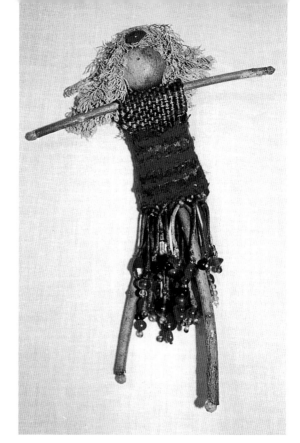

■ Annie Wylde-Beem, *Tina Turner,* 9 inches, chenille and satin cords, beads, and found material. Photo by Annie Wylde-Beem.

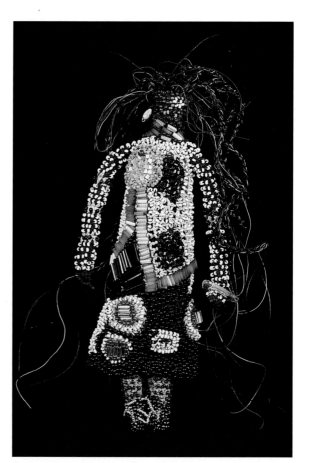

■ Olga Dvigoubsky Cinnamon, *Between Black and White,* 12 inches. Photo by Olga Dvigoubsky Cinnamon.

Free-form /woven—For loose areas such as a sleeve or skirt, beads may be stitched and then woven together right on the figure.

Paper Bead

Magazine pages can make very colorful beads.

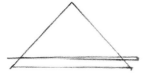

1. Cut a triangle of paper and apply light coat of white glue.

2. Roll paper over a needle or thin stick.

3. Pull out needle.

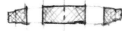

4. Use sharp knife to cut shapes as desired.

■ Karen L. Whitney, *Serena the Mermaid*, 4¹/₂ inches, wooden case and wooden head bead covered with seed beads and shells.
Photo by Patti Burris.

■ Janet Kay Skeen, *Angel Puss*, 10¹/₂ inches, (left) and *Yvonne, She Dances Badly* (right), 13 inches, painted and painted muslin.
Photo by Ken Sanville.

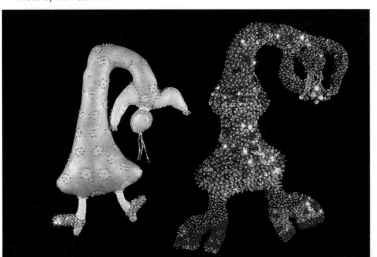

■ Barbara McClean, *Fred,* 9 inches, beaded, rollled felt. Photo by Barbara McClean.

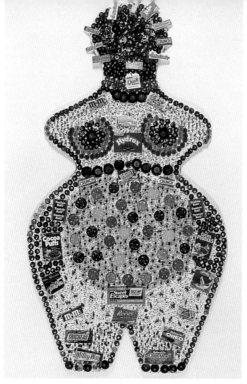

■ Lynne Sward, *Goddess of Chocolate,*
16 inches, fabric, colored photo copies,
bead and sequins.
Photo by Dave Wilson.

■ Lynne Sward, *My Mother the Domestic Goddess,*
13 inches, fabric, charms, yarn, photocopy, vinyl.
Photo by Dave Wilson.

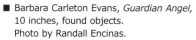

■ Barbara Carleton Evans, *Guardian Angel,*
10 inches, found objects.
Photo by Randall Encinas.

■ Annie Wahl, *Traditional Dress,*
15 inches, Super Sculpey.
Photos by W. Donald Smith.

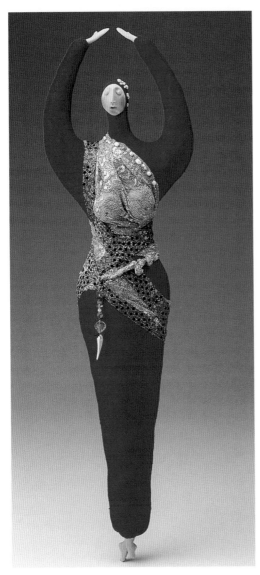

■ Barbara Morrison, *Frosting Fetish with Sprinkles,*
12 inches, polymer clay, mixed media.
Photo by Patrick Clark.

■ Gretchen Lima, *The Chakra Goddess,*
25 inches, cloth, Sculpey.
Photo by Bill Lemke.

■ Andrea Stern, *Fetish A-Go-Go,*
8 inches, crochet and beadwork.
Photo by Andrea Stern.

■ Barbara Johnston, *Ikati Molwani,*
16 inches, cloth.
Photo by Les Bricker.

■ Lisa Lichtenfels, *Cardinal Angel,*
25 inches, nylon needle-sculpture.
Photo by Lisa Lichtenfels.

CHAPTER SIX

Specialized
Costume

Wings

Flights of Fancy

Wings, tails, and pointy ears are things that really belong to the body or form of a figure and as such need to be considered during its design and construction. Even though they may be applied, you might want to be thinking about how they will be applied over (or through) a finished costume. Or, if they will be a part of the costume fabric. Always ask yourself if the style and shape of the wing you chose will "go with" the doll.

A simple stuffed shape seems to call for wings made of the same material with stitched embellishment.

These fluffy feathery wings just don't seem like they would really lift this figure.

A firmly stuffed, chubby-shaped cloth doll would seem to go best with a stuffed wing. However, on a realistic sculpted piece, that same wing would look "unflyable." After all, the wing is an extension of the body.

Where do you get ideas for wing and tail shapes? Storybooks with fairy tale and fantasy illustrations are a good place to start. Also, check out design pattern books such as the Dover series books and natural history sources such as nature magazines and books.

Fabric wings can usually be made and sewn on after the figure has its costume. They are usually two pieces of fabric sewn together, turned and stuffed, sometimes stiffened with wire or fabric stiffeners such as liquid or iron-on interfacing, and then embellished with paint, dye, or machine embroidery. But not always. Some very interesting wing and tail designs for stuffed fabric dolls can be made by using fabric manipulation tricks like layers of prairie points or other two-piece sewn and turned shapes. Virginia Robertson's *Wings* booklet covers many of the variations of shape and construction one might think of for this type, so lets look at a few other methods.

Many doll makers have worked out variations on two methods of wired wings. In the first method floral wire (paper-covered 30-36 gauge wire, lengths are bent to form the upper edge of a wing with a loop at the inside end for attachment. The loop can be used to sew wings to the figure's costume or it can be thickened and twisted, and inserted into a hole prepared for it in a sculpted body.

■ (Above) Annie Wahl, *Tau Moth,* 9 inches, Super Sculpey. Photo by Lloyd Wilson.

■ Olga Andrianova, *Muse,* 40 cm, fabric. Photo by Victor Chernishov.

Diane Keeler sketches her desired wing shape and covers the sketch with plastic kitchen wrap. Over the covered sketch she places a piece of wing material—often silk or organza. Wing edges and interior segments or (struts) are outlined with a bead of Fabri-Tac! and the wires are glued in place over the glue lines. A layer of fusible heat bond fabric is sandwiched between the wired layer and a top layer and ironed to fuse the two layers. Excess fabric is cut away. If this method is used with silk, you can paint or dye the wings in delightful shadings to match your figure's costume.

Sue Canelli has used horsehair cord sewn between two layers of organza with a double needle to make a realistic mermaid tail. This would be a good method to try when making large wings or tails requiring more strength. My much more simple approach to a mermaid tail was to gather silk chiffon and cut it to form a tail "V" shape, then fringe the ends to add to the feeling of a tail floating in water.

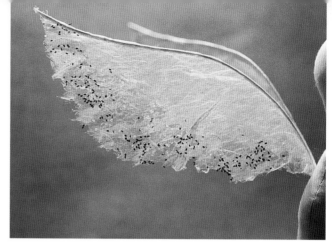

■ Jane Houck, *Flower Fairy* detail, 18 inches, cloth. Photo by Isaac Bailey.

Jane Houck's Method I: Draw a design on handmade paper. Cut the shape allowing $1/8$-inch or less for a folding allowance.

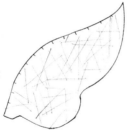

Snip the folding edge to allow it to fold around curves.

Run a bead of white craft glue along the upper edge of the wing, lay the wire along the folding line and bring the folding allowance over the wire and glue in place. For extra strength, glue additional wires to the paper to outline wing segments. Jane decorates her wings with glittery paints, odd scraps of laces, and paper cut-outs. She often tears the lower edges of the wings to achieve an extra fluffy feathery look.

■ Jane Houck, *Flower Fairy*, 18 inches, cloth. Photo by Isaac Bailey.

Method II:

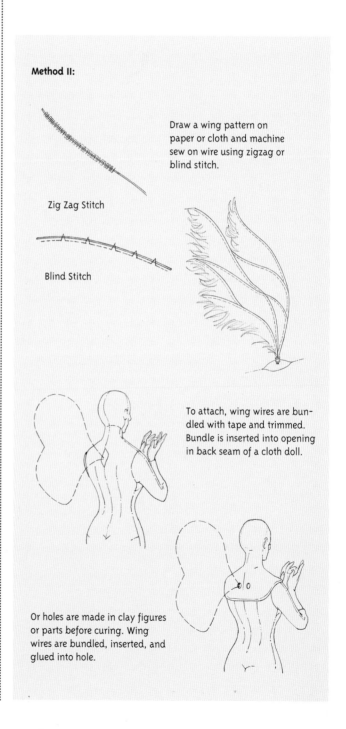

Draw a wing pattern on paper or cloth and machine sew on wire using zigzag or blind stitch.

Zig Zag Stitch

Blind Stitch

To attach, wing wires are bundled with tape and trimmed. Bundle is inserted into opening in back seam of a cloth doll.

Or holes are made in clay figures or parts before curing. Wing wires are bundled, inserted, and glued into hole.

■ Annie Wahl, *Owl Moth,* 13 inches, Super Sculpey. Photo by W. Donald Smith.

Feather wings — Some craft suppliers carry actual preserved bird wings. Here, you want to consider how they will be connected and if they might be a bit too heavy or out-of-scale for your piece. The alternative to a purchased feather wing is one you make yourself by cutting out a shape and gluing the feathers on one at a time. Tedious, but probably worth the effort if the look requires it.

Butterfly wings — Craft suppliers also carry look-alike moth and butterfly wings which are actually made from feathers.

Wired fabric wings — These are usually in pastel colors, sometimes with white printed designs, and made of wire that's covered with a stretchy nylon-stocking-type mesh. Since they are only infrequently found, here is a way you can make your own:

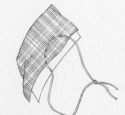

Wire 1: Bend wire into loops. Take an 8 x 8-inch square of very sheer nylon stocking material and fold it over the loop. Pull gently so as not to bend wire and gather excess fabric into your hand.

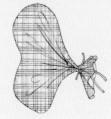

Holding excess at twisted end of loop, stitch or wrap thread around gathers to secure. Adjust wire to keep fabric in tension. Insert into figure. Use excess fabric as part of the decorative "fluff" on the back of your figure.

Wire 2: It's fun to create filmy wings with fabric or feathers, but why not just suggest a wing by bending aluminum sculpture wire or brass wire into curly shapes. Sometimes juxtaposing very different materials can help underscore a unique message. Here, the metal provides the feeling of lightness and glitter and other-worldliness.

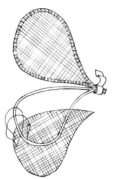

Wire 3: Use either rod or wire to create desired shape. Whipstitch fabric to frame or apply very light, thin coating of glue to wire and lay on silk or chiffon fabric. When glue is dry, trim excess fabric to the wire. Paint with watercolors or brush on dye.

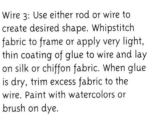

These wings are made from aluminum sculpture wire, simply bent and shaped by hand. The loose and abstract lines highlight the idea of airiness and floating.

■ Anne-Marie Brombal, *Butterfly Fairy Rosie,* 22 inches, Fimo and paper clay. Photo by Anne-Marie Brombal.

■ Jane Houck, *Skyletta,* 22 inches, cloth.
Photo by Isaac Bailey.

■ Julie McCullough, *Smoke and Shadow,*
27 inches, velvet and netting.
Photos by John Nollendorf.

■ Margery Cannon, *Star Tender,*
30 inches, cloth.
Photo by Jan Shue.

■ Jane Darin, *Initiates Dance,* 24 inches, cloth.
Photos by Werner Kalber.

■ Sherry Housley, *Bird Goddess,*
16 inches, mixed media.
Photo by Sherry Housley.

■ Jane Davies, *Ice Fairy in Spring,*
12 inches, paper mâché.
Photo by Jerry Anthony.

■ Sandra Thomas Oglesby, *Giving You Joy is My Only Thought*,
10 inches, polymer, movable wings.
Photo by Sandra Thomas Oglesby.

■ Martha Boers and Marianne Reitsma,
Butterfly Monarch, 14 inches, Super Sculpey.
Photo by Marianne Reitsma.

■ Annie Wahl, *Moth on Moth Balls,*
 12¹/₂ inches, Super Sculpey.
 Photo by W. Donald Smith.

■ Annie Wahl, *Lunar Moth,*
 11 inches, Super Sculpey.
 Photo by W. Donald Smith.

■ Sandra Thomas Oglesby, *Orbit,*
 13 inches, polymer, movable hand-painted wings.
 Photo by Sandra Thomas Oglesby.

Glasses: Windows on the World

Eyeglasses—most of the population over 50 wear them, many others as well. Some characters are just going to require them. The easy way out might seem to be commercially manufactured doll or teddy bear glasses. Some are quite nicely fashioned, but except for the larger toy dolls, they are very much out of scale. To bring them into scale would require removing the lens part and substituting a much thinner piece of clear Mylar.

But don't deny yourself the fun of creating a truly unique pair of glasses to enhance a character. Choose one or more of the methods shown to develop a basic frame. From there, keep the character in mind and use your own imagination to add finishing touches.

■ (Above) Jane Darin, *St. Agnes Academy is Having a 40th Reunion* detail, 24 inches, cloth.
Photo by Joe Darin.

■ Chris Chomick and Peter Meder, *Magda,* 12 inches, Cernit.
Photo by Jason Marsh.

Method 1

Similar to Chris Chomick and Peter Meder's Method.

Roll out a $1/8$-inch thickness of polymer clay.

Draw or trace glasses shape on clay and cut out. Glue side/temple pieces to front or bend to make wraparound frames.

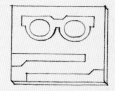
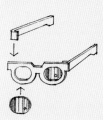

Cut and glue clear plastic (Mylar) to inside of frame to make lenses.

Method 2

For a round frame, you need a fine wire, probably 20-gauge, a pair of round-nose pliers and a wood dowel or pen the circumference of the lens you want. Find appropriate forms among your scraps and tool handles to make oval or rectangular shapes, or bend "by eye."

Wrap wire one time around form. Remove from form and bend over round pliers to make nose bridge. Put wire against form and bend for second half. Be sure to bend so that the wire comes over on the same side as the first half.

Form side pieces separately and hook to front. Use flat nose pliers to squeeze side pieces tightly together at connection.

Put on doll and trim ends of side pieces so they fit over ears. You might want to consider drilling a tiny hole behind the ear to receive the wire side piece. (Less likely to fall off and be lost that way.)

 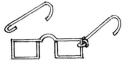

If side pieces are not flattened tightly, glasses will be loose. A small drop of hot glue or liquid solder at the connection will help keep side pieces rigid.

Method 3

Jane Darin's Method:
Make front frame as in method 2. Use separate wire in one continuous run to make side piece and decorative front top.

Method 4

Annie Wahl's Method:
Start by folding 15 inches of wire in half.

Cross the two halves at the middle and twist to make bridge.

Place a felt tip pen or pencil at one side of bridge between wires and twist the wire on the opposite side. Repeat for opposite side. This makes front lens part of frame.

Continue twisting wires to make side pieces. Use the pliers to flatten the whole piece. Use pliers to shape front lens piece as desired. Bend side pieces back.

Decorate by applying glue to front part of glasses. Glue can be painted or used as a base for sequins, beads, or other metallic trims.

■ Nancy Cronin, *Santa's Glasses*, 5 inches, Porcelite edition. Photo by Nancy Cronin.

Other glasses hints:

■ Mary Ellen Frank uses watch crystals for eyeglass lenses.

■ Use colored or metallic, and/or glittery hot glue to make abstract shapes.

■ Use plastic strips which can be softened in hot water to form frames or decorations.

■ Try hammering/embossing designs in copper or metal sheets available at craft or model-making suppliers.

■ To secure to a fabric doll, make loop at end of side piece. Sew through loop to attach to head behind ear.

Note: When photographing dolls wearing glasses, take time to play with the pose and camera angle so that the eye itself can be seen through the lens opening. Sometimes full front or full profile is the only successful way to allow the character's eyes to be seen.

■ Diana S. Baumbauer, *After the Recital*, 18 inches seated, cloth. Photo by Diana S. Baumbauer.

Jewelry

The Finishing Touch

Jewelry often completes and adds just the right finishing touch to a costume. If it does, then your main consideration in design is making it look like it belongs to the figure. For realistic figures, you will want to make delicately detailed pieces scaled to the figure. For abstract or character dolls, you might think of big, bright, and exciting pieces.

To make or to remodel human-scaled jewelry parts, you will need two or three pairs of pliers—round nose, wire cutting, and snippers. You will also need a supply of jump rings and chain in various sizes and metallic finishes and all the old jewelry parts you can get—brilliants or unset stones, possibly small earrings for pierced ears. Also, jewelry glue. I stress parts because most doll jewelry is or should be re-assembled so that it looks like it was created for the doll.

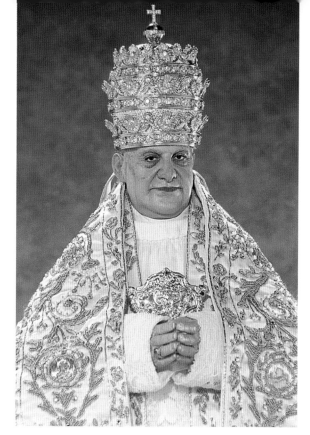

■ George Stuart, *Pope John XXIII,* 18 inches, Super Sculpey, mixed media. Photo by Peter D'Aprix.

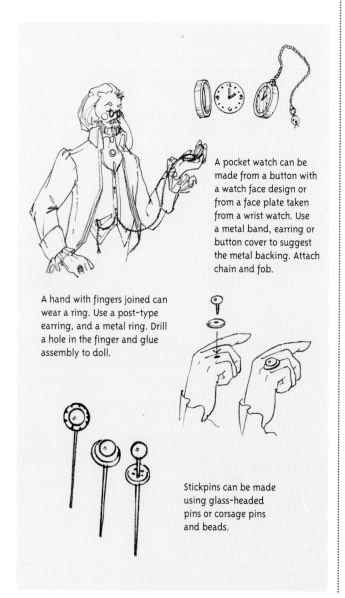

A pocket watch can be made from a button with a watch face design or from a face plate taken from a wrist watch. Use a metal band, earring or button cover to suggest the metal backing. Attach chain and fob.

A hand with fingers joined can wear a ring. Use a post-type earring, and a metal ring. Drill a hole in the finger and glue assembly to doll.

Stickpins can be made using glass-headed pins or corsage pins and beads.

■ Chris Chomick and Peter Meder, *Nina, Vocals the Kamakzi Squirrels,* 12 inches, Cernit. Photo by Jason Marsh.

Sculpted dolls can wear any type of pieced design you can imagine. Just drill a hole in the ear and glue assembly in. If you know you are going to make earrings for a polymer figure, make holes before curing.

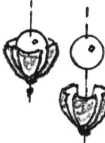

Metallic bead holders can make ring bases—or fairy crowns.

Use an assortment of charms and the spacer from a necklace to make a chatelaine.

■ Michelle Robison, *Mystic Warrior,* 12 inches, glass clay. Photo by Michelle Robison.

Bracelets can be made of washers, earrings, or jewelry findings. Make them colorful by wrapping with cord or yarns.

Very delicate jewelry can be made by assembling chain and beads with jump rings.

■ Karan Schneider, *The Nightmare,* 21 inches, Crea-Therm and Cernit. Photo by Studio Rossi.

Animals

A Doll's Best Friend

Many of us see our figures finished with accessory pets or stuffed animals. However, it's often impossible to find something to purchase that fits the figure in scale or finish. Most of the time, you will find it far more satisfactory to make a good matching piece yourself. Making it yourself really completes the figure and makes the whole thing a total design of your very own.

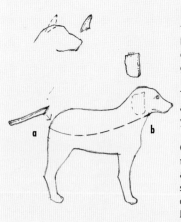

1. Find a side view drawing of the animal you want to make. Dictionaries, encyclopedia or children's picture books are good sources.

Trace the outline of the animal and enlarge it to the height you want your figure to be.

Cut out the outline of the animal's body shape, minus ears and tail. These will become separate pattern pieces. The outline cutout will be the side-body pattern piece.

Lay the paper side-pattern piece on a second piece of paper and trace around the legs to chest and tail. Draw a line following the profile of the stomach and chest. This will become the tummy gusset piece. Note: most four legged animals are wider in the chest area between the front legs.

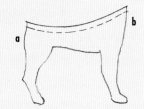

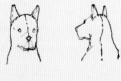
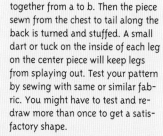
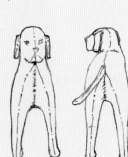

Cut 2 gusset pieces and sew them together from a to b. Then the piece sewn from the chest to tail along the back is turned and stuffed. A small dart or tuck on the inside of each leg on the center piece will keep legs from splaying out. Test your pattern by sewing with same or similar fabric. You might have to test and re-draw more than once to get a satisfactory shape.

■ Diana Lence Crosby, *The Fairy Equiana and Mr. Maple Magic,* 18 inches, wooden articulating body covered with cloth. Photo by W. Donald Smith.

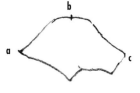

Most outline head shapes will expand sufficiently when stuffed to form the desired animal shape. If the head is extra wide—as with a bear— you might want to create a separate head piece with gusset for added forehead width.

Use outline form to draw and cut ear and tail pattern pieces. Hand sew them on.

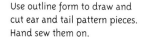

A tail can be reenforced with a piece of pipe cleaner or chenille stem.

Hedy Katin, *Dovey with Dogs,* 10 inches, fabric. Photo by Hedy Katin.

Hedy Katin is noted for making furry animals with paint and batting. She begins the dog by making an armature of pipe cleaner. Polyester batting muscles are applied to the armature to fill it out and then the fur is sewn on to fit the built-out form. The final touch is painting any exposed polyester batting areas such as the muzzle and paws. Since it has a wire framework, it is somewhat poseable.

Pose

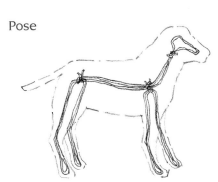

If you want your animal to be poseable, make a simple armature of wire and insert it before stuffing.

Noses

1. Shiny black noses can be made by modeling black polyform clay (Fimo/Sculpey) and coating it with polymer (acrylic) lacquer after baking. Attach clay noses with glue. You can do hooves the same way.

2. A sewn on button can become a nose.

If legs are long, you might want to consider inserting a simple wire armature for reinforcement. Leave opening between tail and upper hind leg for stuffing. Animals with more specific muscle definition can be built over a wire armature wrapped with polyester stuffing and/or strips of batting. If the animal is to be made in a non-woven material such as felt, you can hand-sew pieces with an overcast or blanket stitch.

Eyes

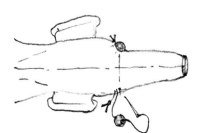

Eyes can be small beads or domed buttons, or purchased animal eyes. If eyes are sewn on, you can pull thread so that the bead or button makes an indent as if it were in an eye socket.

For eyelashes, knot thread leaving a tail behind the knot. Take a small stitch in and out of the head where the eye is to be placed. Pick up a bead on the needle and sew through the head to other eye area. Pull thread to make eye socket indent. Secure thread and repeat for the other eye. The knot and thread tail define the eye corner and make a tiny eyelash.

Finishing suggestions:

- Use mohair fleece or fuzzy yarns to create furry finishes.
- For shorthaired animals, sew the body of felt and use appliqué to create "pinto patches" and/or colored pencils and pens to sketch in suggestion of hair.
- Whiskers: Broom straw can be threaded on a needle and pulled through nose area.
- Materials: Experiment with fabrics such as vinyl and velvet that reflect animal hides and coats. Consider creating your figure in woven cotton and then painting it if you want the hide effect. Fake fur fabrics are often too large in scale to make good doll-sized animals—and just as often far more awkward to deal with. Give fake furs "haircuts" with scissors or razor to grade pile into a good scale. Or make the animal from felt or low pile fabric, cut hair from fur or fur fabric and glue it on the animal in small pieces—just enough to suggest fur. Fill areas between glued fur by sketching fur lines with felt pens.

■ Robert Cunningham, *Crane Rider,*
78 inches, Super Sculpey and wire armature.
Photo by Jan Pisarczyk.

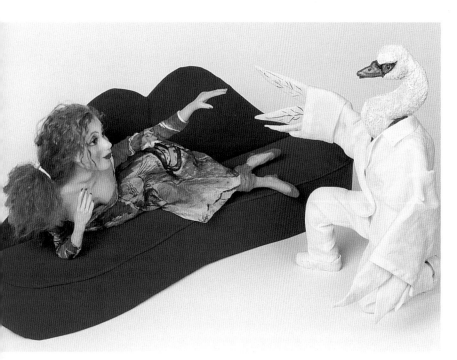

■ Anna Avanesova, *The Romance of Leda,* 24 cm,
Fimo and Super Sculpey.
Photo by Victor Chernishov.

■ Ima Naroditskaya, *Who Are You?,*
12 inches, La Doll and textile.
Photo by Elena Polosukhina.

■ Martha Boers and Marianne Reitsma, *Gnome on a Dragon*,
19 inches, Super Sculpey, fabric over wire armature.
Photo by Chris Crossley.

■ Marlaine Verhelst, *Fighting the Clouds*,
16 inches, direct sculpted porcelain and paper mâché.
Photo by Marcel Teuns.

■ Marlaine Verhelst, *Riding a Rhinocerous*,
20 inches, direct sculpted porcelain and
paper maché. Photo by Marcel Teuns.

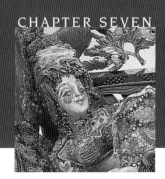

CHAPTER SEVEN

Display

We doll makers have a large streak of the illustrator in us. We tend to see our figures against a backdrop—either real or imagined—and we want to bring this scenery to life as well. If we make Cinderella, we want to make the castle and the coach, too. These ideas require painting a picture in 3-D with the appropriate props. Some ideas will actually require props. "Mary, Mary" without some suggestion of a garden won't truly communicate the rhyme. In most cases, when we want to show Alice's Tea Party, we have to make the table, chairs, teapot, and cups as well as the March Hare, Mad Hatter, and Dormouse. This means more things to make and to integrate into a well-designed whole.

Therefore, sometime in the early conceptual stages of your design, you will be giving thought to where the figure will live, what it will live with, and how you want it to be seen, appreciated or judged. This means display. It means deciding what type of doll it will be—an art piece, an interior decoration, or an interactive play piece.

Art pieces are usually fairly static. They, like sculpture, are mostly fixed into place on a stand or a base and they may or may not have a setting. Dolls made for decoration or a little more casual living are a bit more movable. They can sit on a bed, be propped in a window, stood on a shelf with collectibles and curios, or be part of your seasonal decorations. Interactive dolls are dolls that children or adults can manipulate. If toys, they will be totally transportable and dependent on the child's imagination. If made for adults, the interactive piece will deserve some sort of space in a place where it can be accessible to the player.

Considerations

Typically, the three common methods of displaying a figure are: to stand it up in a purchased metal doll stand, to place it in a piece of doll furniture, or to attach it to a stick, a wood or metal rod inserted into a wooden base. All of these work, but they might not add much to the piece to make it an interesting whole. When you design your piece and as you work, consider how it will show to its best advantage.

Of course, not all figures need traditional bases. Some can fly from the ceiling, hang from the curtain rods, some can live in special boxes, and some can just sit or stand all by themselves.

The doll as an art piece should be meant to be seen from all sides unless a backdrop is part of its setting. Don't forget about the back and sides—at the gallery it might be placed on a free-standing pedestal. This might mean that it needs to be on a base that a viewer can move. It also means that external supports should be blended into the setting or kept so that they do not detract from the piece and its personality. Another important consideration for the art piece is transportation and set-up. Can you pack this piece? How will a museum staff or gallery owner set it up? Will they be able to set it up to be seen as you want it?

■ (Above) Barbara Chapman, *Narcissa on Love Seat* detail, 16 inches, silk-covered wire settee. Photo by Bob Hirsch.

■ Nancy Wiley, *White Snake,* 60 inches, painted cabinet with painted canvas background, paper clay figures. Photo by Robert O'Brien.

If your figure is to be sold, you will need to present it in such a way that the potential collector can see it easily as part of his environment. You want him to say, "This figure could hang in my entry, this doll could sit on my bed, or this doll would make a great feature on a pedestal in my living room." You don't want the potential buyer to say, "I love this doll, but I can't think where I could put it."

The figure should be well attached to things that go with it. It doesn't take long for an important object to get separated from the figure. Make sure hats are sewn or glued on (I have had to make three hats for a doll that kept losing hers). Loose items can be sewn or glued to the hands or bases or even attached by using an "invisible" nylon filament or a fishing line or thread. Dolls can be sewn, tied, or wired onto their chairs or their pillow props. Send your pieces out with photos or instructions about pose and accessories. I carefully packed the teacup that went with one of my dolls by placing it under her. The museum staff looked high and low for it, but never found it. She sat on that teacup for the whole three months of the exhibit.

Props, accessories, and settings should be constructed with an idea of making the piece last intact for as long as possible. All things, including dolls, will degrade with age, but with care in assembly, they could easily last a century or two. Parts should not be easily breakable. You should also be careful about organic things such as dried flowers, which might disintegrate over time.

Cleaning for most pieces will be done with a duster, brush, or a covered vacuum. Be sure to assemble your piece so that it can be easily cared for. Consider bell jars, cases, or acrylic covers if the piece has many small dust-catcher accessories.

Dolls that sit or stand by themselves should be weighted or designed so that they will not topple at the slightest puff of air. Cloth or polymer stand-alones can have BBs, copper

shot, or fishing weights built into the feet during construction. Dolls that sit can be given a weight-bag filled with the same or with plastic doll pellets. (Don't use anything organic that will rot or attract rodents and do not use metals that will rust in humid areas.)

Needless to say, props and setting should go with and complement the figure and its statement, not overwhelm it. We usually always want the viewer to see the figure first and then be able to evaluate it or react to it as it works in its setting.

Materials

Traditionally, figures are pegged into a base of round or square wood. Some are pegged into pieces of solid glass or acrylic. Lazy Susan turntables and scrap pieces of resin counter-top materials can also be used. Bases can suggest environment: painted seashore, carpet, forest floor. Don't forget that dolls can also be containers or be put in containers such as Althea Church's "cake" below or, the traditional jack-in-the-box, or traveling dolls, with wardrobes, trunks, suitcases. Dolls can be made to be seen in fancy presentation boxes or dolls are often put in frames such as Ellen Rixford's *Victorian Family*.

■ Althea Church, *Too Much of a Good Thing*, 12 inches, cloth. Photos by Lee Webb.

■ Hennie Koffrie, *Queen of Nothing*,
12 inches, paper clay, woven metal.
Photo by Charisma, Germany.

■ Barbara Redemer, *Beach Beauty*, 13 inches, fabric.
Photo by Bonnie Stockton.

Display Ideas

Wood: Consider decoupage blocks, shelves, frames, boxes, assorted wood shapes from thrift stores, garage sales, and craft suppliers. Lumberyards will cut hardwood blocks for you. Pre-finished wood bases (plaques) may be found at trophy shops.

Glass / acrylic: Most glass suppliers can cut any shape for you in glass or acrylic. Comparatively, acrylic is expensive and it is difficult even for a professional to drill especially close to the edges. You can bend acrylic material with home materials, but results may be uneven. Best to have it done to order. Look for acrylic tissue boxes, desk organizers, and box-shaped photo frames.

Unusual forms: Try baskets and basket-woven shapes and containers, such as boxes and steamer baskets. Also try circuit boards, wood, or plastic cutting boards, cheese boards (with glass or plastic domes), rock and rock-like products such as counter-top materials of pseudo granite (cabinet makers often have sample-sized pieces as well as scraps). Use lazy Susan revolving wood base, old shoes, suitcases, vases, candelabra, etc.

Natural materials: Driftwood, barn boards and the like should be used with caution. Be sure pieces are dry, clean, and bug-free. Add clear sealer for additional protection.

Hanging arrangements: Visit lighting shops for decorative and functional ceiling mounts. Visit garden and indoor nursery shops which have wall-mounted hangers. Decorative ornament hangers make good display supports for smaller figures.

Finish: Be sure your base material is clean and smooth on the bottom. Add felt dots to protect fine-furniture display surfaces. Add feet of wooden beads or metal hardware, such as round-shaped drawer pulls.

■ Barbara Chapman, *Baba Yaga,* 20 inches,
paper clay face, cloth over wire armature.
Photo by Bob Hirsch.

Furniture — Four Ways

Just about every person involved with figure making is going to spend a little or a lot of time thinking about the construction of things found and used in our environments—from airplanes to computers. After clothing, the next problem to come up is often furniture for the figure. A chair, a sofa, or a bed. Real or fantastical? Soft, hard, or a combination?

If you have a wood shop and the ability to use the tools, you would simply make furniture by making miniatures of the real household pieces. However, most of us do not want to make small-scale wooden furniture and most of us do have access to a sewing machine, fabric, cardboard, and glue—the main ingredients for making doll furniture in the sewing room. After that you need a good verbal description (or a drawing you make) of a piece of furniture you want to make.

Finishes: Use silk flowers, tole painting, painting soft-stuffed furniture, adding paper clay or paper mâché to build up decorative areas, woven seats and backs. Try different styles of weaving, different materials for weaving such as plastic bags, felt strips, wire, using nail heads or upholstery tacks for decorative embellishments.

■ Yolanda Barona, *Aunt Mildred*, 14 inches seated, Premo polymer clay.
Photo by Lyle Van Koughnet.

■ Susanna Oroyan, *Maymee Roundheels*, 10 inches seated, polymer clay.
Photo by W. Donald Smith.

Ideas for furniture:

- rolled and cut corrugated paper
- rolled felt cylinders
- fabric stiffener used in a shape-and-drape manner
- wrapping wire. How many different things could be used for wrapping?
- cardboard tubing, plastic containers, fast-food containers, soft drink bottles
- spools, wood craft pieces, popsicle sticks, chopsticks

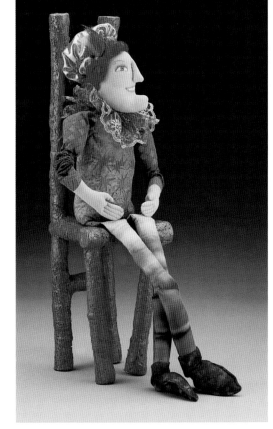

■ Deborah Spanton, *Prince in a Chair,* 18 inches seated, chair constructed of cloth, wire, corks, and plastic. Photo by Bill Bachhuber.

■ Michael Langton, *Neil and Gail,* 18 inches seated, carved and joined wood.
Photo by Jerry Anthony.

■ Susanna Oroyan, *Poppy,* 16 inches, polymer clay.
Photo by W. Donald Smith.

128 | FINISHING THE FIGURE

1

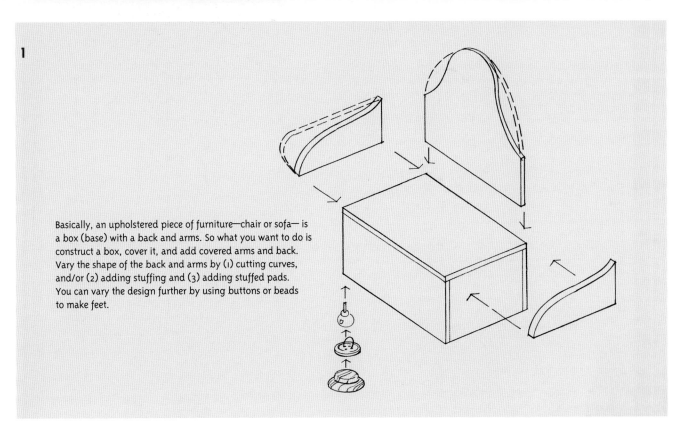

Basically, an upholstered piece of furniture—chair or sofa— is a box (base) with a back and arms. So what you want to do is construct a box, cover it, and add covered arms and back. Vary the shape of the back and arms by (1) cutting curves, and/or (2) adding stuffing and (3) adding stuffed pads. You can vary the design further by using buttons or beads to make feet.

2

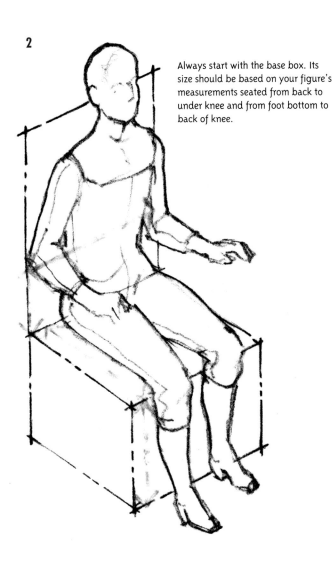

Always start with the base box. Its size should be based on your figure's measurements seated from back to under knee and from foot bottom to back of knee.

3 Check measurements because dolls are often longer in the legs than you think...you don't want the knees under the chin, or the legs sprawling out, do you? If your figure is four inches from foot bottom to knee, your box needs to be at least three inches high. The other inch of height will be gained by the addition of a chair cushion and feet on the furniture. If your figure is five inches back to front, the sides of your base should be five inches. Next measure your figure across from elbow to elbow to get the width or size of the back and front pieces.

4

Be sure to weight your figure by adding pellets or clean pebbles inside the body at the bottom and in the feet. The weighting will make the figure "sink" and sit more naturally.

The furniture pieces you might have in your home are constructed of wooden frames covered with fabric stretched and nailed onto the wood framing. Covering cardboard or foamcore with fabric is the easiest way to simulate real-world furniture without resorting to the wood shop. If you want precision depth, cardboard shapes should be given a wood or foam-core spacer.

1

Upper Front

fold

fold   fold

fold

Lower Front

A simple folded cardboard chair. You will probably see several ways this could be varied by adding arms, or slanting the back, or re-cutting to create legs.

Cut patterns of cardboard. Cover cardboard with fabric (double fabric and make pocket for seat front and lower back upright as shown).

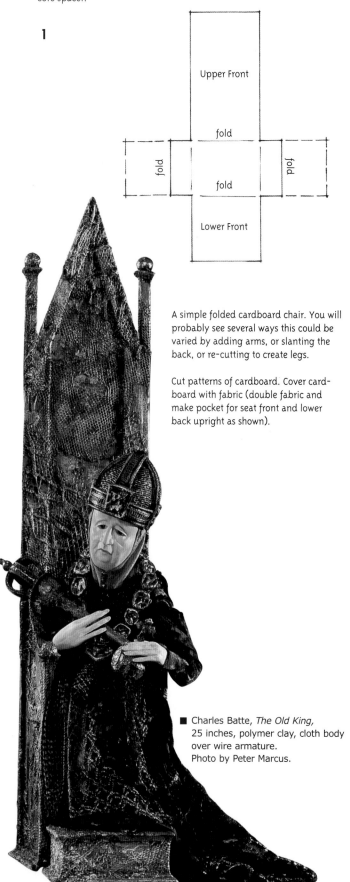

■ Charles Batte, *The Old King,*
25 inches, polymer clay, cloth body over wire armature.
Photo by Peter Marcus.

2

Fold into chair position and sew seat sides to front and back

Back

3

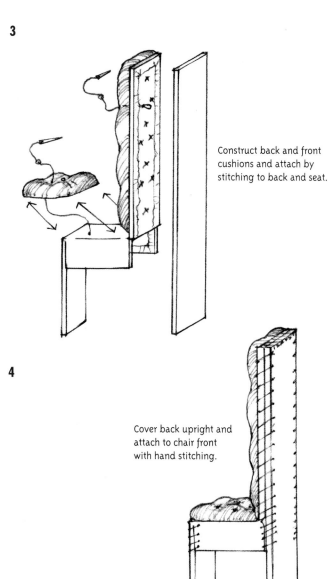

Construct back and front cushions and attach by stitching to back and seat.

4

Cover back upright and attach to chair front with hand stitching.

■ Elizabeth Brandon, *Saturday Night at the Pla-Mor,*
14 inches, porcelain.
Photo by Jerry Anthony.

Wing Chair

1

Here is a summary of *Sitting Pretty* a pattern I designed for a wing chair. I started by constructing a six-piece seat box. The box pieces were covered by gluing or sewing fabric to the cardboard and assembling the pieces with hand stitching.

2

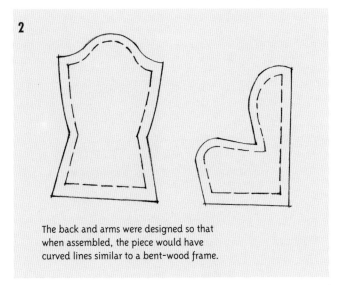

The back and arms were designed so that when assembled, the piece would have curved lines similar to a bent-wood frame.

3

I used the cardboard back and arm pieces to make patterns for cutting fabric. After sewing and turning the pieces, I slipped them over the cardboard pieces and added a thin layer of batting cut to the same shape as the cardboard pattern. Raw edges were turned under and sewn closed.

Then the cardboard back and side pieces were pinned together and assembled by using an overcast stitch.

4

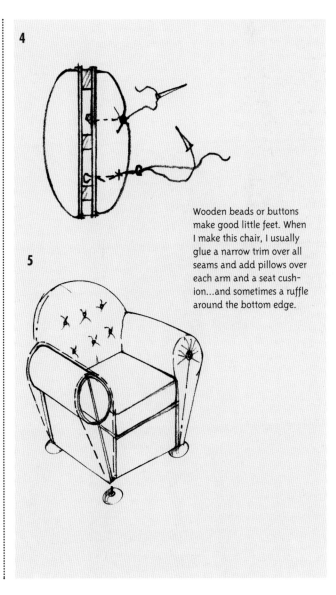

5

Wooden beads or buttons make good little feet. When I make this chair, I usually glue a narrow trim over all seams and add pillows over each arm and a seat cushion...and sometimes a ruffle around the bottom edge.

The Soft Seat

For the people who like sewing and stuffing, here is another way:

1

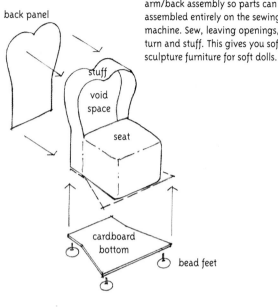

back panel

stuff

void space

seat

cardboard bottom

bead feet

General Method

Measure and develop pattern pieces. Add spacer strips for width if desired. Make separate pieces for inside of arm/back assembly so parts can be assembled entirely on the sewing machine. Sew, leaving openings, turn and stuff. This gives you soft sculpture furniture for soft dolls.

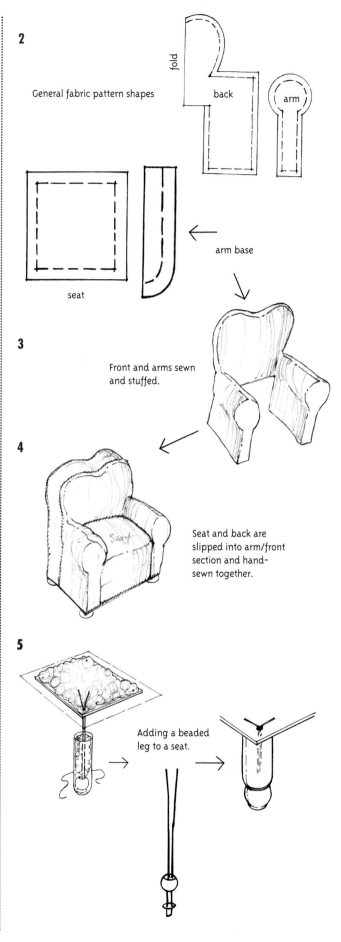

2

General fabric pattern shapes

fold

back

arm

seat

arm base

3

Front and arms sewn and stuffed.

4

Seat and back are slipped into arm/front section and hand-sewn together.

5

Adding a beaded leg to a seat.

■ Marcella Welch, *Wind Spirit,* 38 inches. Photo by Marcella Welch.

Structuring Soft Shapes

A Built-Up Form

If you don't mind a mess, try a paper mâché chair built on cardboard tubing.

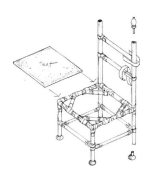

Here, tightly rolled and taped cylinders of newspaper are taped together and covered with bulk paper mache product (wet newspaper strips will also work).

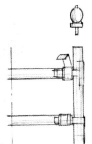

Wood beads or buttons can be used to add decorative touches.

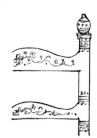

Note that you can also use plaster-saturated gauze (cast material) or dampened cotton buckram to build up a form.

A Wire Frame

For the more avant-garde, try a bent wire frame like this. Weave interesting fibers through the wire or wrap it.

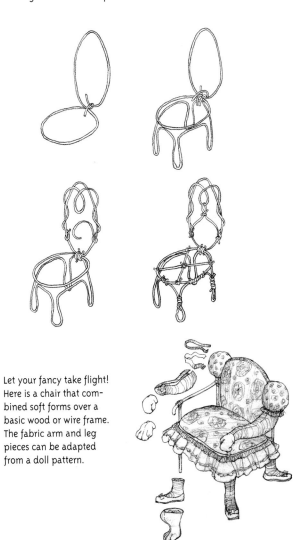

Let your fancy take flight! Here is a chair that combined soft forms over a basic wood or wire frame. The fabric arm and leg pieces can be adapted from a doll pattern.

■ Ginger Roberts, *Interlude*, 11 inches, paper clay. Photo by Ken Worrow.

■ (Right) Rita Keizer, *The Troll Counselor*, 12 inches, nylon over wire armature. Photo by Rita E. Keiser.

■ Jolene Thompson, *Mother Earth*,
16 inches, Super Sculpey.
Photo by Robin Foley.

■ Martha Christman, *The Muffins,* 7 inches,
nylon stocking over Dacron stuffing.
Photo by Martha Christman.

■ Ima Naroditskaya, *Origami,* 6 inches, La Doll.
Photo by Viktor Chernyshov.

■ Ludmila Ovchinnikova, *Nobody Knows How Much I Had to Overcome*, 50 cm, textile. Photo by Viktor Chernishov.

■ Ima Naroditskaya, *The Wishing Tree,* 16 inches, La Doll. Photo by Elena Polosukhina.

■ Ima Naroditskaya, *Autumn,* 18 inches, La Doll. Photo by Elena Polosukhina.

■ Linda Kertzman, *My Mommy Makes Bears,* 26 inches,
Cernit, Super Sculpey.
Photo by Jack Cole.

■ Mary Jo Carpenter, *Spiral Bound,* 19¹/₂ inches,
Super Sculpey.
Photo by Mary Jo Carpenter.

■ Mary Jo Carpenter, *The Great Escape,* 14 inches,
Super Sculpey over wire armature.
Photo by Mary Jo Carpenter.

■ Rita Carl (Reets), *Spooky Tooth,* 22 inches,
muslin/sandcastle-cotton.
Photo by Douglas Beck.

■ Judith S. Klawitter, *Paul, the Bristol Butcher,*
22 inches, Super Sculpey.
Photo by Mark Bryant.

■ Martha Boers and Marrianne Reitsma, *The Jimson Weed,*
doll 14 inches, easel 18 inches, Super Sculpey, wire, cloth body.
Photos by Marrianne Reitsma.

■ Kathryn Walmsley, *In the Garden,* 15 inches,
Cernit, wood and paper clay.
Photo by Jerry Anthony.

CHAPTER EIGHT

Beyond

We all know stories of doll makers who magically make their pieces become living beings. In the real world, artists do not have that kind of fantastical ability. They do, however, work toward making their characters vibrate with life as much as possible with materials and process available or invented. They are ever on the alert for new technologies which will enable them to take you to new places and meet new people and ideas in their work. In the end, finishing the figure means endowing it with qualities that will engage the viewer and provide him with something to appreciate, think about, or even play with. Any well-done piece provides a surprise and the challenge to be understood, appreciated, or at least experienced by the viewer.

The part of the creative process where the artist interacts with the concept of character is unquestionably the key to creating a successful figure. What you see in the static figure is, for the artist, only a moment in the life and world of her imagined character. Although she only shows you an abstracted moment, in the artist's mind the figure exists as a total personality, with a life history and a unique environment. More artists are choosing to show these elements or parts of them in new, non-traditional forms and modes. This often brings us to a point where no lines of definition are possible. Nor are they necessary. An object does not have to be typed or named for engagement.

Artist Ellen Rixford has taken the traditional clockwork automata ideas and combined modern electronics to create figures that can show several aspects or moods of one persona. When she does that, is the result a doll, a mannequin, or a mechanical device? We don't have to know to be fascinated with the personality aspects it reveals as it moves.

All doll makers immediately recognize the element of dollness and, perhaps, an element of their souls in the work of Sha Sha Higby (below). She becomes the doll. Sha Sha literally makes it live.

How do these artists—we might call them the avant-garde—finish their figures? The same way any other artist does. They find a vision. They think about what needs to be done (technical work) to make it happen (design). They study traditional forms and consider how they can be used or changed or reconstructed in their vision (study, experimentation, and practice.) If a material they need does not exist, they often create it (invention). They do hours and hours of painstaking work to make every part of the work as perfect as it can be. If the result is not the expectation of the viewer, that is simply because these artists are not afraid of re-defining the edges of the known doll world. They enjoy it as much as the traditional artist enjoys perfecting a figure with known processes and commonly found materials.

In the end, fabricated figures, art dolls, mixed media sculpture— whatever you call them, whatever type you like, whatever type you do, traditional, contemporary, avant-garde—all require the artist to do all that needs to be done to complete the vision as a tangible object. Every time an artist is true to her vision, the knowledge and experience in the world of the maker and the world of the viewer are bettered.

■ (Above) Axel Lucas, *Untitled detail,* 21 inches, porcelain, carved wood.
Photo by Axel Lucas.

■ Sha Sha Higby, *Folded Under A Stone Sleeping,* 70 inches, costume for performance art inspired by bark on trees, made with Japanese lacquer, hemp, wire, and tulle.
Photo by Albert Hollander.

■ Sha Sha Higby, *Cows Under A Pepper Tree,* 70 inches, costume for performance made with Japanese wood and paper techniques, sewing and wood carving. Photos by Fred Mertz.

In the last two decades, animation done with multiple graphic cells moved to the more complex stop-action filming of dimensional figures. Bill Nelson's figures are used to make computer scans to create video animation. What we see on the screen is not the actual figure. It is one way of realizing the maximum potential of the figure.

 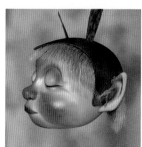

■ Bill Nelson, *Odie,* a Super Sculpey figure used for computer-generated animation. Photo and wire animation graphics courtesy of Main Street Film and Animation.

■ Pamela Hastings, *The Queen of the May Embraces Her Darker Self,*
15 inches, cloth, quilting.
Photo by Allen Bryan.

■ Donna May Robinson, *My Primavera,* 29 inches,
all cloth with oil-painted face.
Photo by Jerry Anthony.

■ Pamela Hastings, *The Queen of the May Ignores Her Darker Self,*
15 inches, cloth, quilting.
Photo by Allen Bryan.

■ Axel Lucas, *Untitled,* 21 inches,
porcelain, carved wood.
Photo by Axel Lucas.

■ Marlaine Verhelst, *Marabou Jail,* 60 inches,
porcelain and paper mâché.
Photo by Marcel Teuns.

■ Ellen Rixford, *Lady of the Inner Light,* (two views of the
mechanical movement), 36 inches, mixed media.
Photos by Ellen Rixford.

■ Dmitry Zhurilkin, *The Vision*, 18 cm, splint, fabric.
Photo by Victor Chernishov.

■ Dmitry Zhurilkin, *The Woman with the Head from Roses*,
34 cm, splint, fabric.
Photo by Victor Chernishov.

■ Gary Wang, *Untitled*, 24 inches,
paper clay, mixed media.
Photo by Gary Wang.

■ Uwe Haukenfers and Juergen Peper, *Oberon*,
16 inches, wood.
Photo by Charisma.

■ Ron Shattil, *Mazel,* 7 x 10 inches, fabric, beads.
Photo by Ron Shattil.

■ elinor peace bailey, *Tokyo Contained,* 22 inches, cloth.
Photo by Isaac Bailey.

■ Ron Shattil, *Hachma,* 10 inches, fabric.
Photo by Ron Shattil.

■ Gail Lackey, *Ingywook,* 9$\frac{1}{2}$ inches, poly form.
Photo by W. Donald Smith.

■ Lawan Angelique, *Madonna* pin, 3 inches,
wired ribbon, metallic trims, found materials.
Photo by Chris Florkowski.

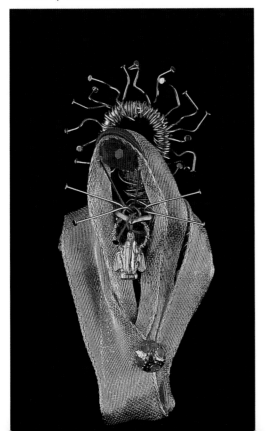

■ Sandra Thomas Oglesby, *The Law of Perfect Balance,*
14 inches, polymer clay and cloth.
Photo by Sandra Thomas Oglesby.

CHAPTER NINE

Photography

For the Record

You might be able to write your own rules for creating your pieces, but there are real, outside, "other" rules for doll photography. And you must follow the rules if you want others to appreciate your dolls in books and magazine articles, buy them or invite them to be seen in gallery competitions. You must.

A photograph is a tool. It is not the real thing. But it has to be as close to the real thing as possible. It cannot leave room for the viewer's mind to fill in the blanks. It cannot show more in the picture than is really part of the piece. That's cheating. Therefore, the first rule of photography is: Nothing is in the picture that does not belong to the piece. Don't take pictures in the garden with flowers; don't take pictures on the coffee table with candy dishes and doilies; and don't take pictures against your upholstered furniture, draperies, or outside against walls or decks.

Use a solid paper, cardboard, or fabric drape that goes behind and continues under your piece. Solid means no wrinkled sheets or fabrics, no bent cardboard or paper, no artful draping of background fabric. It means clean and sharp. If you can take three days and thirty dollars worth of fabric to make a dress for the doll, you can take thirty minutes to press and stretch a fabric or three dollars to buy cardboard or a piece of felt for the photo background.

The only time you might vary from this rule is when you want to style a doll in a setting to make an illustration such as for a storybook or greeting card where the whole picture, not the doll, is the message.

The next major consideration is focus. Here the rule is: All parts of the figure from base to top of head and from back to front must be in sharp focus. If the figure looks fuzzy, the viewer might think the surface is that way. This may mean you have to manually focus, wear your glasses to focus, move back from the figure, and shoot with the camera lens parallel to the figure.

The most important part of getting good focus is understanding how depth of field and focal plane work. Depth of field means the part of the piece that will be in focus. Depending on light, your camera lens and the distance from it to the object, that depth can range from less than one-eighth of an inch (eyes in focus, nose not) to two or three inches. Depth of field also cuts through the figure. If your lens is turned to look up at the doll's face, more than likely its feet will be out of the focal plane. If you focus on the face of a doll that sits, often most of the legs will be outside the field of focus. Turn that doll slightly to the side and move the camera back. It is better to have a small image, well focused than a filled frame out of focus. Keep your lens aimed straight at the piece, focus, using your eye to check through the view finder to be sure all parts outside the focus circle are sharp (getting the part inside the circle focused does not automatically make the whole in focus). Remember, the more light you can use, the sharper the focus and the greater the depth of field will be.

This brings us to lighting. The rule here is: All parts of the doll should be well lit with no harsh shadows or bright spots. Some photos submitted for this book were rejected because of light streaks, flash shadows, whited-out areas or areas without an edge. If one eye is medium blue and the other is lighter, what will the viewer think? He could think you did it that way and that it is sloppy work when, most likely, you didn't check for light glare. Is he going to see what looks like a lightening flash or is he going to see that you used a piece of metallic tissue lame? Is he going to see a pale blur or is he going to see a face with features? If there are black flash shadows outlined around the figure, how will the viewer know where its edges are?

All of these problems can be solved very quickly by losing the flash. Do not use it. Flash lighting, built-in or attached, is meant for taking pictures of real people at distances of more than four feet. Flash is not meant for taking pictures of art subjects. You don't need professional strobe lighting either. All you need are three metal, clip-on, reflector lights with photo-flood bulbs, two white umbrellas to diffuse light and some chair backs to clamp them onto. Extra highlighting can be done by adding lights that will shine down on the piece or pick up on certain areas. If you sell one doll, you can pay for this and probably have change.

If you must use a flash, cover it with tissue paper to diffuse the light. Tilt the flash, if possible, so the light bounces back onto the doll from the wall or the ceiling.

■ (Above) Anne Mayer Meier, *Knobbykneed Flowergirl* detail, 16 inches, fabric, mixed media.
Photo by Jerry Anthony.

Automatic cameras can sometimes be more trouble than they are worth for the features. Auto focus will focus on the part that is nearest—that might be the end of the nose and if it's a long nose, the eyes might be out of the focal plane. Auto settings will balance for light. That means that the camera will make a light figure against a dark background even lighter in the attempt to balance light and dark areas. With a 35 mm camera, you want to manually set the camera to let in light over a long period of time.

Always bracket your shots. Take one, change the lens opening (F-stop) settings and take another. It would be better to lose two out of three than all the shots on your roll. Professional photographers can shoot a whole roll with varying settings in order to get just one good shot. You will pay your professional a good deal more than the cost of a roll of film.

And then there is pose. Always plan your photo so that the doll projects its persona. If it looks like you didn't care how it was presented, the message is you might be sloppy in other parts. If parts are cut off, then the viewer has to guess if the feet are OK, or if the hands have fingers. If he can't see the face, he is not going to be able to understand its character. If he can't see the whole form, he can't understand what it is doing. If you have made an external stand or use a purchased metal stand, take care it does not show. Move the piece until you can no longer see the upright. Be sure the feet are squarely placed so the doll looks like it is standing, not dangling from the waist grip. Put waist rings under clothing—hiding or minimizing stand uprights should be an initial consideration in your design. Use clear plastic boxes to prop soft, floppy dolls or pin them to a stiff, non-shiny cardboard background. Take some time to think as much about the art of the doll's photo as the art of the doll. It counts.

Some problems, but not that many, happen in photo processing. If your negatives, transparencies or slides are done well, as above, then you should get good results. Sometimes, processors are just sloppy. Always question and never accept work that you think is not as good as your negative or slide.

How many and what kind? Your doll is not done until you have made a good picture of it. Authors and publishers prefer to work with the original slide or transparency or a very high-quality sharp print to make their own scans. Submissions of transparencies (positive image) with studio lighting will usually get first attention. Because they are larger in format they will not lose detail in enlargement. Next best are slides. Slides are usually requested for juried events. Slides are easy to see and file. Shoot two identical slides at a time. This will save you money and give you one permanent back-up and one to use for making copies and prints. Prints, if very good,

will be fine. Just remember to mark the negative or slide right away so you know which is the best to copy prints.

Remember: in spite of all modern mechanics, publishers cannot make a bad photo better...and most likely won't bother if there is something else available. Also, because of their composition, color, detailing, some dolls just do not photograph well.

Your photo work is not done until you get a signed release. You may own the copyright on the doll itself, but the photographer owns the copyright on the picture of it and its use. All photos require a photographer's release to make copies or prints. Every photo in this book has an accompanying release from the artist/photographer or the professional they used. If you have someone else do your photos—even your brother— be sure you have him sign a release at the same time. You don't want to lose a chance to be in print because you can't locate a photographer. Always keep file copies of your releases; send duplicate copies to editors or authors.

If the photo is used for publication, always credit the person who did the photography—even your brother-in-law.

Last, but not least, the photo itself needs to carry pertinent descriptive information. It should look like this:

Name of artist: M. J. Dollmaker

Title of piece: Santa's Revenge

Height of doll: 18 inches

Sculpture medium: Super Sculpey over wire armature (or cloth, or paper clay, etc.)

Special details: Beard of braided mohair, hand embroidered details on costume.

Photographer name: John Popshot

For prints and plastic transparency covers, this information can be typed on a label and stuck on. Always tape over the label to keep pen, printer or typewriter ink from smearing and rubbing off on the face of the photos above or below it in a stack. Never write directly on the back of a print as pen and pencil marks will dent the photo surface and make it unprintable. Don't trust a keyed list for descriptions. Lists get lost.

Always remember, your doll is not done until you have a good picture of it and a signed release from the photographer allowing you to use the picture.

CHAPTER TEN

Packing
and Shipping

I would rather make any ten or even a hundred dolls than pack one to be shipped. This may be why I tend to make what I call the Ultimate Unpackable Piece. However, most of us will want to send our figures off to new owners or exhibits. We will have to face the packing problems and we should face them very early in the design process. It will take on-going thought to place even the simplest form in a box. Over the years, I have shipped and received a number of dolls so let me tell you from my own observation what will work best.

There are some basic things to consider when you design. Negative answers to these questions don't mean that you should give up on a complicated design. It just means that you need to consider how to design for transportation.

■ Can the piece come apart, can it be separated from its base and accessories?

■ Are there parts of the piece that will crush or get out of shape if packed ?

■ Will the person who receives the piece be able to put it together and set it up with the exact look that you gave it?

■ When the piece is finished you need to consider the mode of movement. Will you ship this via postal service or package carrier? Will you be carrying the piece in your personal luggage on public transport?

Let's state three rules for all cases:

RULE ONE: Any sort of packing should avoid putting pressure on a piece.

RULE TWO: The piece should be packed so that it cannot move around in the box during shipping.

RULE THREE: Never, ever ship any item in loose Styrofoam pellets. They make a dreadful mess in your house and they will make a mess where they are unpacked. An owner, gallery owner, or exhibit builder is going to hate your piece if it makes a mess he has to clean up. Furthermore, pieces packed in loose Styrofoam "float" during shipment. What you thought you placed in the middle of the box will probably end up on the side or bottom where it can take damage. When you get pellets, immediately bag them in soft plastic. Dry cleaner bags or soft plastic used for vegetables at the grocery store are best. Staple bags to make pellet pillows.

These will adjust themselves around your form and contain the mess.

To comply with those rules the best interior packing materials will be:

■ Plastic pellets well-captured in soft plastic bags

■ Fixing the piece to a solid panel of cardboard or hard insulation

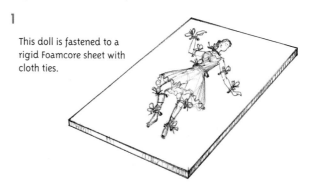

This doll is fastened to a rigid Foamcore sheet with cloth ties.

■ Encase in a specially hollowed out piece of solid Styrofoam with or without soft finger foam.

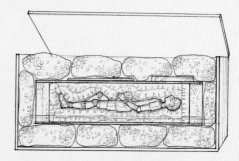

This doll is packed in a box made of rigid Styrofoam and Foamcore sheets. The doll is held in place with pieces of finger foam. The whole package is placed in a covered cardboard box lined with bags of Styrofoam pellets. Note that the base is packed separately on top of the inner box. Set-up instructions should be taped to the top of the inner box so they can be immediately seen.

■ Julie McCullough, *Smoke* and *Shadow* detail, 27 inches, cloth sculpture, velvet and netting. Photo by John Nollendorf.

■ Encase in finger foam and placed in a hard-sided (dent-proof) container.

3

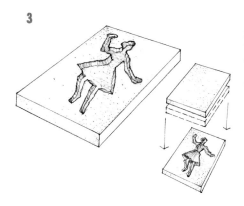

Sketch the outline of your doll on a piece of 2-or-3 inch rigid Styrofoam insulation. Then, hollow out a space for it to lie in. If the figure has more depth, hollow out a covering piece of foam. Add small bits of foam rubber to keep doll from shifting, if necessary (#1 above).

Soft finger foam upholstery or mattress material can be found at some fabric stores and most upholsterers. Hard Styrofoam panels used for building insulation can be purchased at builders' supply. Cut or saw the panels to needed sizes. Laminate panels if more width is needed.

The best exterior packing will be a cardboard box in excellent or new condition, with flaps that cover the opening entirely. Commercial shippers routinely require double boxing for any dolls you want treated as fragile items. That means a second box that fits exactly inside the first or that has a layer of packing material (paper, bagged Styrofoam pellets) between the interior and exterior boxes. Interior boxes can be built of Styrofoam panels. The basic idea is that when they throw the tractor tire on top of your box in the mail truck, your box can withstand the weight without crushing the interior box.

As you can see, packing requires special materials. These are costly and should be figured into the price of your piece or the shipping fees. This is what "handling fees" are. These are separate from actual shipping costs and are a definite part of your business expense.

■ Jill Hamilton, *Lailoken*, 21 inches, paper clay head, cloth body. Photo by Jill Hamilton.

Preparing for packing: Take pieces off their stands or bases if possible. Do this especially in cases where breakable legs are pegged into bases. Wrap a decorative base in the same way you would a doll. Use the pellet bags or foam rubber and secure the piece so it cannot move around. Always pack bases away from/separated from the dolls. Remove any held or attached accessories such as hats, walking sticks, baskets, or toys. Pack these in a separate box and plan so that it can be placed in your main shipping box without being able to move or push into your doll figure. In some cases a doll in a chair can be packed as one. When doing this I "mummy" wrap the whole piece with kitchen plastic wrap.

When you take a piece apart to pack it, you must provide specific written instructions for unpacking—which parts to remove first—and its set-up on the receiver's end. This should include a photo of the piece as it should be seen. Also include instructions for care and cleaning. Your instructions should be on letterhead or with your address and the address of the receiver. Put all written material in an envelope and pack it so that it is the first thing seen when the box is opened.

Example 1 Porcelain or breakable material. If the piece does not have a number of parts that stick out in all directions, the best mode will be to encase it in a Styrofoam mold case. Some shippers offer "blown-in" foam packing. The piece is wrapped in plastic and hot liquid foam is blown into the box forming a solid mold around it. It can't move and it can take pressure.

Example 2 Breakable piece. Here you use the Styrofoam panel material to hollow out a top and bottom. The doll is placed in the hollow case. To prevent movement within the case, a layer of soft finger foam (mattress or upholstery material) can be put over the doll.

Example 3 Breakable piece. If the piece is relatively flat, it can be laid against a Styrofoam panel and tied down. Use a long bodkin needle to punch cloth tie material through the panel. Don't use wire as it can "saw" on both doll and panel. The sides of the panel can be built up with a lip higher than the highest part of the piece and a lid placed over the top.

Example 4 Tie down. This is the one that can go in "open air" and it will work for soft, light-weight cloth, wire-armatured pieces. Here the piece is suspended within the box, or its base is secured to the bottom of the box. No other packing is added.

Example 5 Soft cloth. This seems like an easy one because it can't break. But skirts or wings or jointed limbs and molded faces could crush. Your goal is to pack it so that it is as crispy when it comes out of the box as when it went in. More simple stuffed figures can be bagged in plastic and laid in a box between plastics bags filled with stuffing or plastic pellets (cookies, peanuts, shells, etc.) Put a layer of thin foam rubber or folded paper under skirts and between petticoats and skirts. This will help avoid wrinkling. Use white paper—newspaper can make ink smudges. Wrap the head with kitchen plastic wrap to keep hair styles in order.

Traveling with your dolls: Many of us take dolls to shows or conferences in our luggage. Unless your pieces are all soft cloth, you will need to have hard-sided luggage. For instance a 28-inch Pullman rolling suitcase can hold up to ten fragile dolls packed between layers of finger foam. Rolling, hard plastic storage boxes are also a good consideration. I line one side of the open case with finger foam, lay the dolls so that hands or extending parts rest between the foam fingers, then cover the whole with another layer of finger foam. This keeps pieces very securely in place. Your main concern is to check very carefully so that when the case is closed, the foam will not press down on any part of the piece and put it under pressure.

Modes of shipping vary. Essentially, you want the safest, fastest, and most economical. Pay a little extra for air and/or first class. Be sure you have registered or certified mail or shipping tracking number in case a package must be traced. Make some calls to find out which modes are available in your area and in the receiver's. Commercial shippers often require a street address for delivery. Talk with the receiver about the best way for him to get your package. He might prefer to make a drive to a shipping center or post office rather than have a package left on his doorstep or roadside mailbox. Also note that when you use commercial shippers, they can pick up packages at your door, thus saving you the hassle of carrying and standing in lines with large boxes.

Shipments going overseas may require import duty fees to be paid by the receiver. Ask your addressee how he wants value stated. Shipments going overseas for exhibit (and being sent back to you) will require special paperwork or you will be required to pay import duty on your own pieces to get them back. Talk to your shipper about specific requirements. Usually, this will require three copies of a notarized letter describing the purpose of the shipment (for exhibit at museum X and the dates) accompanied by three copies of a photo of the piece.

Insurance: Technically, the piece belongs to the buyer and is his responsibility the minute he buys it. However, insurance claims must be filed by the shipper: you. Claims for full value may result in the freight company or post office keeping the piece. If the piece can be fixed, you might want to file a claim for part value to save the piece from a damaged goods auction or the garbage.

■ Jane Darin, *Self-portrait—Feeling All Untied,* 24 inches, cloth. Photo by Werner Kalber.

The Artists

If you write to the artists, please enclose a stamped envelope for their reply.

Angelique, Lawan, 2458 W. Bayshore, #7, Palo Alto, CA, 94303

Anzai, Akiko, 1609 Treehouse Lane, Roanoke, TX, 76262

Armas, Pamela, 3435 Texas Street, San Diego, CA, 92104

Austin, Sara, 4035 Stalwart Drive, Rancho Palos Verdes, CA, 90275

Bailey, Elinor Peace, 1779 East Avenue, Hayward, CA, 94541

Barona, Yolanda, 1217 Franklin Drive, Port Orange, FL, 32119

Bates, Jeanie, 8957 SW Arapaho, Tualatin, OR, 97062

Batte, Charles, NIADA, 272 Divisadero St, #4, San Francisco, CA, 94117

Baumbauer, Diana, 1716 Melbourne Road, Lafayette, IN, 47904

Belzer, Kathryn, 12943 HWY 224, RR2, Schubenacadie, Nova Scotia, BON 2HO Canada

Bibb, Pattie, 247 Overlook Drive, Chulota, FL, 32766

Blythe, Stephanie, NIADA, P.O. Box 1806, San Anselmo, CA, 94979

Boers, Martha and Marianne Reitsma, 1890 Parkside, Pickering, Ontario, LIV 354, Canada

Boyce-Franklin, Alinda, P.O. Box 1518, Mariposa, CA, 95338

Brandon, Elizabeth, NIADA 5916 W 53rd, Mission, KS, 66202

Brombal, Anne-Marie, 8312 Halkin Drive, Plano, TX, 75024

Calhoun, Lynne A. and Debbie McCullough, 4430 N. Rockcliff Place, Tucson, AZ, 85750

Cannon, Margery, 910 Donner Way #204, Salt Lake City, UT, 84108

Carl, Rita, Box 578, Miranda, CA, 95553

Carlson, Jane, 29853 Troutdale Scenic Drive, Evergreen, CO, 80439

Carpenter, Mary Jo, 2721 Bach Avenue, Portage, MI, 49024

Casey, Jacqueline, 1930 Blairsville Hwy, Murphy, NC, 28906

Cely, Antonette, NIADA, 3592 Cherokee Road, Atlanta, GA, 30340

Chapman, Barbara, 353 Glenmont Drive, Solana Beach, CA, 92075

Charlson, Gillie, 8 Bolton Road, Adlington, Nr. Chorley, Lancs, PR 9NA, England

Chomick, Chris and Peter Meder, NIADA, 5248 52nd Avenue, St. Petersburg, FL, 33709

Christman, Martha, P. O. Box 63, Boyds, WA, 99107

Church, Althea, 38 Hancock Street, Arlington, MA, 02174

Cinnamon, Olga Dvigoubsky, 1158 W. 23rd Street, Upland, CA, 91784

Clements, Jan, PO Box 108, Yackandandah, Victoria, 3749, Australia

Collins-Langford, Jan, 607 Bedfordshire Road, Louisville, KY, 40222

Cowart-Rickman, Pamela, NIADA, P.O. Box 602, Rock Hall, MD, 21661

Creager, Richard and Jodi, NIADA, 14704-B Gold Creek Court, Grass Valley, CA, 95949

Crees, Paul and Peter Coe, 124 Alma Road, Bournemouth, Dorset, BH91AL, England,

Cronin, Nancy, 76 Andover Street, Wilmington, MA, 01887

Crosby, Diana, NIADA, 1728 Steele Road, Griffin, GA, 30223

Culea, Patti Medaris, 9019 Stargaze Ave, San Diego, CA, 92129

Cunningham, Robert, 40 McGee Ave Apt 510, Kitchener, Ontario, N2B 2T3, Canada,

Darin, Jane, 5648 Camber Drive, San Diego, CA, 92117

Davies, Jane, NIADA, Amber, The Street, Walburton, Arundel, W. Sussex, BN18 0PH England

Doucette, Robert, 12846 Woodbridge Street, Studio City, CA, 91604

Dudley, Martha Ann, 3039 Four Oaks Drive, Atlanta, GA, 30360

Esslinger, Dru, Rt 2 Box 630, Madison, KS, 66860

Evans, Barbara Carleton, 132 Poli Street, Ventura, CA, 93001

Ewing, Linda, 10736 Darling Road, Agua Dulce, CA, 91350

Feingold, Sandy, 1752 Gascony Road, Encinitas, CA, 92024

Feroy, Meo, 3121 South 349th Street, Federal Way, WA, 98003

Finch, Margaret and Marta Finch-Koslozky, NIADA, 9 Catamount Lane, Old Bennington, VT, 05201

Fletcher, Dan, NIADA, 4761 Broadway, #2E, New York, NY, 10034

Fosnot, Susan, 322 S. Madison Street, Woodstock, IL, 60095

Frank, Mary Ellen, NIADA, P.O. Box 02137, Juneau, AK, 99802

Garber, Valarie, 920 Hobson Street, Longwood, FL, 32750

Geer, Genie, 9236 Church Road #1046, Dallas, TX, 75231

Goodnow, June, NIADA, 2324 Ashley Drive, Oklahoma City, OK, 73120

Hamilton, Jill, 1481 Cranberry Court, Wixom, MI, 48393

Hanslik, Retagene, 533 Fairview Avenue, Arcadia, CA, 91007

Hastings, Pamela, 161 Wilhelm Rd, Saugerties, NY, 12477

Haukenfrers, Uwe and Juergen Peper, NIADA, AM Kiellortzplatz 116, 22850 Norderstedt, Germany

Hayes, Bronwyn, 18 Molyneaux Place, Ferrer, ACT 2607, Australia

Hennen, Margi, 300 Academy Road, Winnipeg, Manitoba, R3MOE9, Canada

Higby, Sha Sha, P. O. Box 152, Bolinas, CA, 94924

Hoelscher, Cindy, 3047 N. Payne Avenue, Little Canada, MT, 55117

Hoover, Bonnie, 26889 Lakewood Way, Hayward, CA, 94544

Hoskins, Dorothy, NIADA, 1411 Mary Ann Street, Fairanks, AK, 99701

Houck, Jane, 20 Sargent Road, Sandown, NH, 03873

Housley, Sherry, NIADA, 7 Warbler's Nest, Swannanoa, NC, 28778

Huston, Marilyn, 101 Mountain View Drive, Pflugerville, TX, 78660

Iacono, Maggie, NIADA, 2 Raymond Circle, Downington, PA, 19335

Jett, Lori, 716 Byland Drive, Beach Grove, IN, 46107

Johnston, Barbara, 5713 Louise Lane, Austin, TX, 78757

Justiss, Sandra Wright, 720 Maplewood Avenue, Ambridge, PA, 15003

Katin, Hedy, 8 Palm Drive, Yankeetown, FL, 34498

Keizer, Rita, P.O. Box 790, Woodinville, WA, 98072

Kertzman, Linda, 37 West Main, Morris, NY, 13808

Kinsey, Dawn, Box 938, Three Hills, Alberta, TOM 2AO, Canada

Klawitter, Judith, 2303 River Road, Missoula, MT, 59801

Koffrie, Hennie, NIADA, Gen Kvd Heydenlaan 9A 3743KT Baarn, Netherlands

Lackey, Gail, NIADA, 11716 Emerald Road, Nampa, ID, 83686

Lamb, Jaine, 34 Queen Street, Orillia, Ontario, L3V 1B7, Canada

Lampi, Sally, 2261 Beckham Way, Hayward, CA, 94541

Landis, Ruth Kuykendall, 1185 Arroyo Grande, Sacramento, CA, 95864

Langhorne, Helen, 2813 Glen Gary Place, Richmond, VA, 23233

Langton, Michael, NIADA, 9 Boat Club Drive, Stratham, NH, 03885

Laverick, Nancy J., 6517-D Four Winds Drive, Charlotte, NC, 28212

Lewis, Anya, 11 Burnham Street #3, Somerville, MA, 02144

Lichtenfels, NIADA, Lisa, P.O. Box 90537, Springfield, MA, 01137

Lima, Gretchen, 1419 S. 20th, Sheboygan, WI, 53081

Lukas, Axel, NIADA, AM Kielortplatz 116, 22850 Nordorstedt, Germany

Maciak, Heather, NIADA, 387 Glamorgan Cr. SW, Calgary, T3E 5B7, Canada

Main Street Film and Animation, 1800 W. Main St., Richmond, VA 23220

McCullough, Julie, 719 P Street, Lincoln, NB, 68508

McGarry, Priscilla, 21 Monadnock Drive, Westford, MA, 01886

McLean, Barbara, 66 East 9th Street, #1915, St Paul, MN, 55101

Meier, Anne Mayer, 124 Broadmoor Drive, Daphne, AL, 36526

Morrison, Barbara, 717 Hiberta, Missoula, MT, 59804

Nelson, Bill, P.O. Box 579, Manteo, NC, 27954

Oglesby, Sandra Thomas, 1160 Glenwood Trail, DeLand, FL, 32720

Oroyan, Susanna, NIADA, 3270 Whitbeck, Eugene, OR, 97405

Patell, Colleen Ehle, 1076 Vernier Place, Stanford, CA, 94305

Paterson, Melinda, 10465 SW Lee Court, Portland, OR, 97229

Patterson, Joyce, 1010 S. Brooks, Brazoria, TX, 77422

Porcella, Yvonne, 3619 Shoemake Ave, Modesto, CA, 95358

Radefeld, Beverly Dodge, 1016 West 6th, Topeka, KS, 66601

Redemer, Barbara, 97 Hermasillo, Sonoma, CA, 95476

Richmond, Debbie, 2401 Bashor Road, Goshen, IL 46526

Rixford, Ellen, 308 West 94th St #71, New York, NY, 10025

Roberts, Ginger, Taproot Drive, Winter Springs, FL, 32708

Robinson, Donna May, NIADA, 17859 Howe Ave., Homewood, IL, 60430

Robison, Michelle, 16316 Road N, Napoleon, OH, 43545

Schneider, Karan, 339 Trumbull Drive, Niles, OH, 44446

Shattil, Deb, 9200 Skyline Blvd, Oakland, CA, 94611

Shattil, Ron, 9200 Skyline Blvd., Oakland, CA, 94611

Shively, Christine, 8717 Hilltop Road, Ozwakie, KS, 66070

Skeen, Janet Kay, 10182 Quivas Street, Thornton, CO, 80260

Smith, Connie, NIADA, 167 Gayle Dr., Gallatin, TN, 37066

Spanton, Deborah, 10655 SW Collina, Portland, OR, 97219

Stern, Andrea, P.O. Box 559, Chauncey, OH, 45719

Stillwell, Tracy Page, 85 Horseneck Road, Warwick, RI, 02889

Strickarz, Ethel Loh, 880 N. Almond Valley Rd, Arkport, NY, 14807

Stuart, George, NIADA, Box 508, Ojai, CA, 93024

Sward, Lynne, 625 Bishop Drive, Virginia Beach, VA, 23455

Thompson, Carla, NIADA, 2002 Roundleaf Green, Huntsville, AL, 35803

Thompson, Jolene, 8605 NE Milton St, Portland, OR, 97220

Triplett, Dee Dee, 10286 Hwy 19 W, Bryson City, NC, 28713

Van der Spiegel, Willemijn, Paardenmarkt 8 6981 AL, Doesburg, Netherlands,

Verhelst, Marlaine, NIADA, Burg. Suysstraat 61 NL 5037 MC, Tilburg, Netherlands,

Wahl, Annie, NIADA, 22275 Penn Avenue, Lakeville, MN, 55044

Walmsley, Kathryn, NIADA, 8041 Shady Road, Oldenburg, IN, 47036

Walters, Nancy, NIADA, 690 Trinity Court, Longwood, FL, 32750

Wang, Gary, 6956 Fremlin Street, Vancouver, BC, V6P 3W4 Canada

Welch, Marcella, 5475 Rte 192, Andover, OH, 44003

White, Alessandra, 805 Dwight St, Ypsilanti, MI 48198

Whitney, Karen, 7954 El Capitan Dr, La Mesa, CA, 91941

Wiley, Nancy, NIADA, 253 Warren Street, Hudson, NY, 12534

Worrow, Mary, 1116 New Jersey Avenue, Altamonte Springs, FL, 32714

Wylde-Beem, Annie, 2943 Apache Avenue, Ventura, CA, 93001

The following artists may be contacted via Irina Myzina, Box #563. C/o IPS, PMB, 666 Fifth Avenue, New York, NY 10103: Adrianova, Olga; Avanesova, Anna; Guseva, Marina; Naroditskaya, Ima; Nasedkina, Elena; Ovchinnikova, Ludmila; Voskressenkaya, Svetlana; Zhurilkin, Dmitry

■ Gary Wang, *Untitled,* 24 inches, paper clay, mixed media. Photo by Gary Wang.

■ (Left) Cindy Hoelscher, *The Dazzling Dancer,* 12 inches, mixed media. Photo by Candice Christensen.

■ Connie Smith, *Virginia Wool,* 12 inches, seated, porcelain and mixed media. Photo by W. Donald Smith.

Bibliography

Books About Costume and Embellishment:

These books may be obtained through your library or its interlibrary loan service.

Ambrus, Victor. *The Folk Dress of Europe.*
Mills & Boone. London, 1979

Baron, Faber. *Color and Human Response,*
Van Nostrand Reinholdt, New York, 1978

Battersby, Martin. *Art Deco Fashion,*
Academy Editions, London 1974

Blum, Stella, Ed. *Everyday Fashions in the 1930s,*
Dover, New York 1986

Bradfield, Nancy. *Costume in Detail, 1730-1930,*
Harrap, London, 1968

Braun and Schneider. *Historic Costume in Pictures,*
Dover, New York, 1975

Buck, Anne, *Dress in Eighteenth Century England,*
Batsford, London, 1975

Coleman, Elizabeth. *The Opulent Era: Fashions of Worth,
Doucet and Pingat,* London, Thames and Hudson, 1990

Contini, Mila, *Fashion.* Crescent, New York, NY, 1985

Dodge, Venus A., *The Doll's Dressmaker,*
David and Charels, 1987

Erickson, Lois, and Diane Erickson. *Ethnic Costume,*
Van Nostrand Reinholdt, New York, 1984

Felger, Donna, Ed. *Bridal Fashions Victorian Era.*
Hobby House, Cumberland MD 1986

Freeman, Sue. *Feltcraft.* David and Charles Croft, 1988

Kohler, Carl. *A History of Costume,* Dover, New York, 1965

Laury, Jean Ray. *Imagery on Fabric,* C&T Publishing,

————. *Photo Transfer Handbook,* C&T Publishing

Laver, James. *Costume Through the Ages,*
Simon and Shuster, New York, 1961

Lewis, Bonnie B. and Mary Ann Kaahunui.
Fabulous Footwear for Fantastic Dolls.

————. *Creating Heavenly Hats for Discriminating Dolls.*

Lee, Sara Tomerlin. *American Fashion,*
Fashion Institute of Technology, New York, 1975

Montano, Judith, *The Art of Silk Ribbon Embroidery,* C&T
Publishing, Concord, CA 1919

Miller, Edward. *Textiles: Properties and Behavior in Clothing Use.*
Batsford, London, 1968

Nunn, Joan, *Fashion in Costume 1200-1980,* Herbert Press,
London 1984

Peacock, John. *Fashion Sketchbook 1920-1960,*
Thames and Hudson, London, 1977

Porcella, Yvonne. *A Colorful Book,* Nissen, Kyoto, Japan, 1986

Probert, Christina. *Hats in Vogue Since 1910,*
Abbeville, New York, NY 1981

Rothstein, Nathalie, Ed. *Four Hundred Years of Fashion,*
Victoria and Albert Museum, London, 1984

Smith, C. Ray. *The Theater Crafts Book of Masks, Wigs, and Make-up,*
Rodale, Emmaus PA 1974

Tate, Sharon Lee. *Inside Fashion Design,*
Canfield, San Francisco, 1977

Tilke, Max. *Costume Patterns and Designs,*
Rizzoli. New York, 1990

Vecellio, Cesare. *Veceillio's Renaissance Costume Book.*
Dover, New York, 1977

Warwick, Edward, Henry Pitz, and Alexander Wyckoff.
Early American Dress, Amaryllis Press 1965

Wilcox, R. Turner. *The Dictionary of Costume.* Charles Scribner's
Sons, New York, NY 1969

————. *Five Centuries of American Costume,* Scribner's,
New York, 1963

————. *The Mode in Costume.* Scribner's. New York, 1948

Wolff, Collette. *The Art of Manipulating Fabric,* Chilton,
Radnor, Pa, 1996

Yarwood, Doreen. *World Costume,* Bonanza, New York, NY 1978

————. *European Costume: 2,000 Years of Fashion,* Larrouse
and Co., New York

Sources

Books specifically relating to doll costuming and embellishments, write for catalogs.

Hobby House Press
1 Corporate Drive,
Grantsville, MD 21536

Scott Publishing Company
30595 Eight Mile Road
Livonia, MI 48152

C&T Publishing
1651 Challenge Drive
Concord, CA 94520
www.ctpub.com

Creative Paperclay
79 Daily Drive, Suite 101
Camarillo, CA 93010
www.paperclay.com

La Doll, Premier, Cernit, Flumo
Handcraft Designs
63 East Broad Street
Hatfield, PA 19940
www.hdclays.com

Super Sculpey, Premo
Polyform Products
1901 Estes Avenue
Elk Grove, IL 60007
www.sculpey.com

General Art/Craft Supplies
Sax Arts and Crafts
PO Box 2002
Milwaukee, WI 53021

Dollmaking Supplies
Virginia Robertson/Hard To Find Catalog
PO Box 357
Delores, CO 81323

Mohair
Fireside Basics
PO Box 1000
Missoula, MT 59806

Other products commonly used by the artists whose work is shown are made or distributed by the following: Kunin (felt), Fairfield Products (batting, stuffing), Sulkey Products (metallic fibers), Offray (ribbons), DMC (threads), Delta Technical Coatings (paints). These products can be found in most fabric and craft stores.

■ Barbara Chapman, *Narcissa on Love Seat*, 16 inches, silk-covered wire settee. Photo by Bob Hirsch.

About the Author

Susanna Oroyan taught herself the art of doll making. Since 1972, she has made over 500 dolls, and her doll making has become a full-time career and business. For the past decade, Susanna has been a motivating force in regional and national doll makers's organizations. She has exhibited her dolls internationally, and in 1995 received the Dollmaker of the Year award at the National Cloth Doll Festival. Susanna is the author of *Fantastic Figures*, *Anatomy of a Doll*, and *Designing the Doll*, and has written numerous articles for doll magazines. She has also taught doll making classes at many major seminars as well as for individual doll making groups. Susanna's cloth doll patterns are available from:

Fabricat Designs
3270 Whitbeck Boulevard
Eugene, OR 97405

Other Fine Books by C&T

For more information write for a free catalog:
C&T Publishing, Inc.
P.O. Box 1456
Lafayette, CA 94549
(800) 284-1114
e-mail: ctinfo@ctpub.com
website: www.ctpub.com

For quilting supplies:
Cotton Patch Mail Order
3405 Hall Lane, Dept. CTB
Lafayette, CA 94549
(800) 835-4418
(925) 283-7883
e-mail: quiltusa@yahoo.com
website: www.quiltusa.com

Index

Abstract figure 88

Artists

Other books by Susie Oroyan